Jill Gordon's
Countryside Views in Cross Stitch

David & Charles

A DAVID & CHARLES BOOK

First published in the UK in 2003
Text and designs Copyright © Jill Gordon 2003
Photography and layout Copyright © David & Charles 2003

Distributed in North America
by F&W Publications, Inc.
4700 East Galbraith Road
Cincinnati, OH 45236
1-800-289-0963

Executive commissioning editor Cheryl Brown
Executive art editor Ali Myer
Book designer Lisa Forrester
Desk editor Sandra Pruski
Copy-editor Linda Clements
Photography Stewart Grant and Lucy Mason

Printed in China by Hong Kong Graphics & Printing Ltd.
for David & Charles
Brunel House   Newton Abbot   Devon

Visit our website at www.davidandcharles.co.uk

David & Charles books are available from all good bookshops;
alternatively you can contact our Orderline on (0)1626 334555 or write
to us at FREEPOST EX2110, David & Charles Direct, Newton Abbot
TQ12 4ZZ (No stamp required UK mainland).

Contents

Introduction

This is my second book of cross stitch designs and although my first love used to be painting and then needlepoint, through the creation of these books I have become more and more enchanted with the possibilities of cross stitch.

I was delighted to start working on a book of designs illustrating a variety of international landscapes, although these designs were to be slightly different in that each of the landscapes included a dwelling or building typical of the countryside. Previously I had preferred my landscapes without any sign of human habitation but when it came to actually creating the designs, I became totally fascinated by all the different buildings there are in various parts of the world, and became even more absorbed by the challenge of depicting them in a pleasing way in cross stitch.

Although architecture features strongly in this book, I have also included some favourite flowers and landscapes which has involved the pleasurable task of revisiting old memories of travels across Europe and the Middle East while locating sketches and photographs to use as references. This has made it all a very personal experience and I hope that this comes across in the designs.

I'm sure that you will find the book easy to use – there are twelve cross stitch designs, each illustrated with a large colour photograph of the finished project and accompanied by my own original watercolour sketches for the designs.

The charts are produced in full colour blocks with symbols and are easy to follow. All the projects have a full list of materials needed to complete the stitching and are followed by stitching guidelines. I have used Anchor stranded cotton (floss) to stitch all of the designs because I very much value the colour scope and richness of their range but you will also find a DMC conversion chart at the back of the book if you prefer to use that range. One skein per colour has been used unless otherwise indicated in the chart key.

You will find information on the materials, equipment and basic techniques used in the book on pages 98–103. There are also details on how to work all the stitches and how to make up the designs into a variety of beautiful objects.

I have thoroughly enjoyed the drawing, painting and stitching of all of these projects and I hope that you will enjoy stitching them and making them up as much as I have.

Dutch Windmills

Many different types of buildings are featured in this book and the inclusion of windmills, being such impressive constructions, seemed a natural choice. The ones I most like are these beautiful dark wood and stone windmills, with their elegant ochre red sails. These particular windmills are used in the Netherlands to remove excess water from the polders to the surrounding storage water, but windmills have also been used to grind corn, saw wood, cut tobacco into snuff and pulverize rocks as well.

LEFT *Such a picturesque design as this would make a lovely framed picture or stitch up into a most attractive cushion.*

In a good wind it is said that a large windmill can lift 45,000 litres (10,000 gallons) of water per minute to a height of 1.3m (4ft) – quite a feat. In days gone by, a Dutchman's wealth was often calculated by how many windmills he owned. The fact that people actually lived in windmills was also new to me. Somehow I thought that they were always purely work places rather than dwellings but apparently they were also very cosy and attractive to live in. The décor seems to have been rather like that found in canal longboats – lots of shiny copper and brass and dark green paintwork. The beds were tucked into alcoves rather like shelves.

I was surprised to learn that the windmill is the symbol of the Netherlands – I was sure it must be the tulip. These flowers, the other main feature of this design, have always seemed to represent the country. Dutch tulips are prized all over the world and not so long ago there was all kinds of skulduggery associated with new breeds of tulip bulbs. I have always assumed that tulips are Dutch natives, so it was another eye-opener to find that they are in fact native to Asia and like dry, sandy mountainous regions. It is astonishing the Dutch have been so successful in growing them – to the extent that over half of their 19,000 hectares (47,000 acres) of flower farms are planted with tulip bulbs.

This design sprang into my mind as soon as I had the idea of including windmills and then it was just a question of finding some windmills that appealed and making sketches of great swathes of tulips. Tulips are a wonderfully exotic flower and look very beautiful *en masse* like this. The tulips were lovely to stitch – I always enjoy blending shades and creating the highlights that bring my subjects to life. I thought that this design would make an ideal tray inset and could see it in my mind's eye laden with pretty blue and white Delft china.

Dutch Windmills

Design Size
23cm x 18cm
(9in x 7in) approximately

Stitch Count
124 x 98

Materials

• 33cm x 28cm (13in x 11in)
14-count Aida in Delft blue (Charles Craft 2529)
• Size 24 or 25 tapestry needle
• Anchor stranded cotton (floss) as listed in the key

STITCHING GUIDELINES

Begin by finding and marking the centre of the fabric
(see Techniques page 99). Many stitchers like to begin in
the centre of a design but this is a matter of preference.

The entire design is worked in whole cross stitches
using two threads of Anchor stranded cotton (floss). It is
a good idea to sort the threads on to an organizer before
you begin stitching as this will make work easier. It is
important to buy the shade of Aida fabric suggested, or a
similar shade, because the blue of the material suggests
the water and the sky in this design. Obviously, if
you use a different colour, the end result will also be
quite different.

When the stitching is finished, remove any guidelines
you have used and gently steam iron the embroidery on
the wrong side, taking care not to press too hard as this
flattens the stitches. It helps to place the design face
down on a soft towel before ironing. I have chosen to
make this design up into a tray inset, following the tray
manufacturer's instructions.

KEY
Anchor stranded
cotton (floss)

▮	66
▬	68
◪	69
◩	76
◪	99
◪	212
◪	225
◪	226
●	227
◤	245
↑	265
▬	355
N	831
◄	851
◪	1018
✛	1031
▪	1038
◸	1039
◪	1041
▽	1070
✕	1072
✚	1074
◪	1076
◐	1082
◪	1084
◪	1086
▼	5975

Mexican
Adobe

I have always loved brightly painted houses. This probably dates from childhood and seeing the almost surreal colours of the beach huts that lined the sea-fronts of various seaside towns in which we lived. But, to my eye, they only looked in their right place when the sun was shining and the sea was glistening, its colour incredibly blue. In Mexico, the adobe buildings exude the warmth and gaiety of the climate and this use of colour inspired me to create this design.

RIGHT *This design would be perfect as a picture in a contemporary frame. The colourful border is ideal for decorating many items – for example, you could stitch a section of it for a towel border.*

Adobe is the Spanish word for a sun-dried brick and the clay soil it is made from. It is one of the earliest methods of home building known to man. Interestingly it has been used in one form or another throughout the world, although in Europe it was made from rammed earth rather than adobe bricks, probably because of the lack of sufficient sun to make these dried bricks. The attraction of such buildings for me is the wonderfully individual and innovative use of totally natural materials and the beautiful way in which the dwellings are decorated. The roofs of adobes were also made from natural fibres, sometimes different types of grasses or fan-shaped fronds of palms. These are secured in layers, creating tiny air pockets which act as insulation.

The cacti and succulents that I have used in the foreground are favourites of mine too. The way in which such beautiful plants grow and produce the most exquisite flowers in such unlikely and seemingly arid places, is always a source of surprise and pleasure. It was fun looking at Mexican textiles and experimenting with them until I arrived at the combination of colours that really worked with the design and that I liked. Then I stitched these in, to make the border for this exciting cushion.

Mexican Adobe

Design Size

36cm x 32cm (14¼in x 12½in) approximately

Stitch Count

199 x 175

Materials

- 46cm x 42cm (18in x 16½in) 14-count Aida in warm grey (Fabric Flair 778)
- Size 24 or 26 tapestry needle
- Anchor stranded cotton (floss) as listed in the key

STITCHING GUIDELINES

It would be easy to alter the size of this design by leaving a gap of unstitched fabric between the central picture and the border, so it is important to decide whether you would like to change the size before

beginning. It is also important to leave approximately 5cm (2in) of unstitched fabric surrounding the design in order to be able to make it up into whatever finished project you wish.

You can start stitching wherever you prefer. I enjoyed stitching the house initially and then moving outwards from that. I left the border until the end because it was easy to pick up and stitch at any time as it does not require as much concentration as the actual picture itself.

The entire design is worked in whole cross stitches using two threads of Anchor stranded cotton (floss). It is a good idea to sort the threads on to an organizer

before you begin stitching. It is important to buy the shade of Aida fabric suggested or a very similar shade because the grey of the material suggests the sky, part of the mountains and some of the shadows in the picture and if you use a different colour, the end result will be quite different.

When the stitching is finished, remove any guidelines and gently steam iron the embroidery on the wrong side, taking care not to press too hard as this flattens the stitches. It helps to place the design face down on a soft towel before ironing. I have chosen to make this design up into a cushion and details of this are in Making Up on page 101.

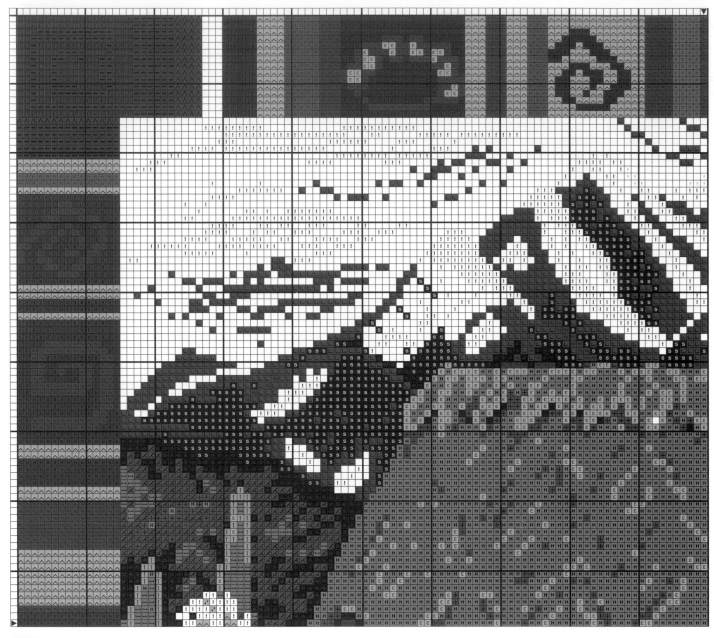

KEY
Anchor stranded
cotton (floss)

! 1	∧ 131	⊢ 266	· 303	✚ 888	∟ 921	∨ 1072
▒ 11*x3*	≡ 142	◤ 267	⌂ 324	H 890 *x2*	S 922	⊤ 1074
▪ 49	⊏ 209	■ 269	⟩ 339	E 891	∿ 1041*x2*	
⊤ 60	↑ 255	∧ 298	■ 877	■ 904	✕ 1070	

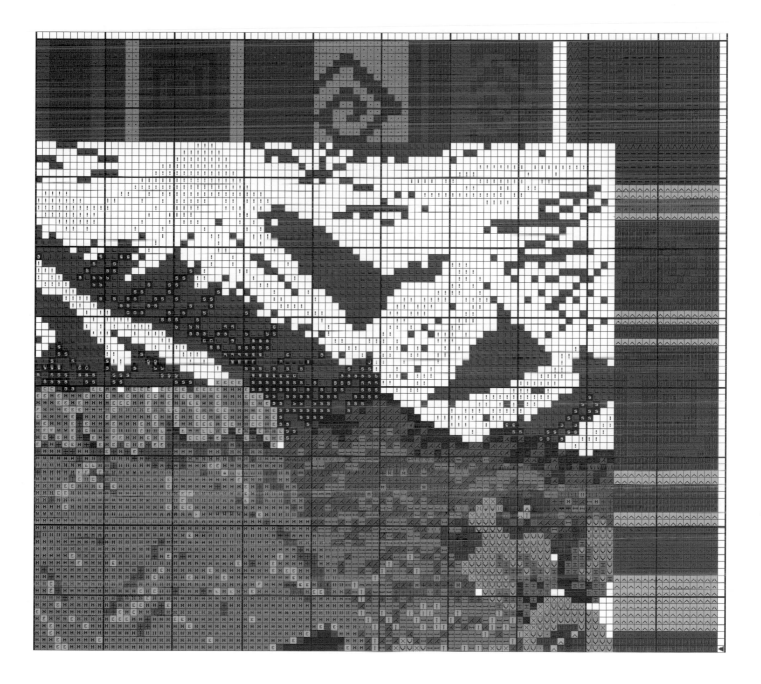

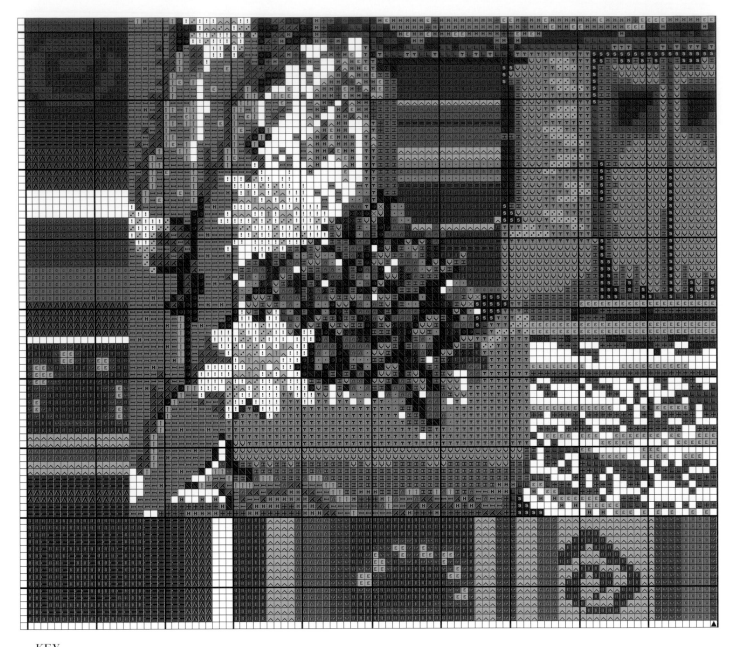

KEY
Anchor stranded
cotton (floss)

! 1	∧ 131	⊢ 266	· 303	+ 888	L 921	∨ 1072
‖ 11 *x3*	= 142	⊠ 267	⌂ 324	H 890 *x2*	S 922	⊥ 1074
▪ 49	c 209	◼ 269	Σ 339	E 891	⋒ 1041 *x2*	
T 60	↑ 255	∧ 298	◣ 877	N 904	✕ 1070	

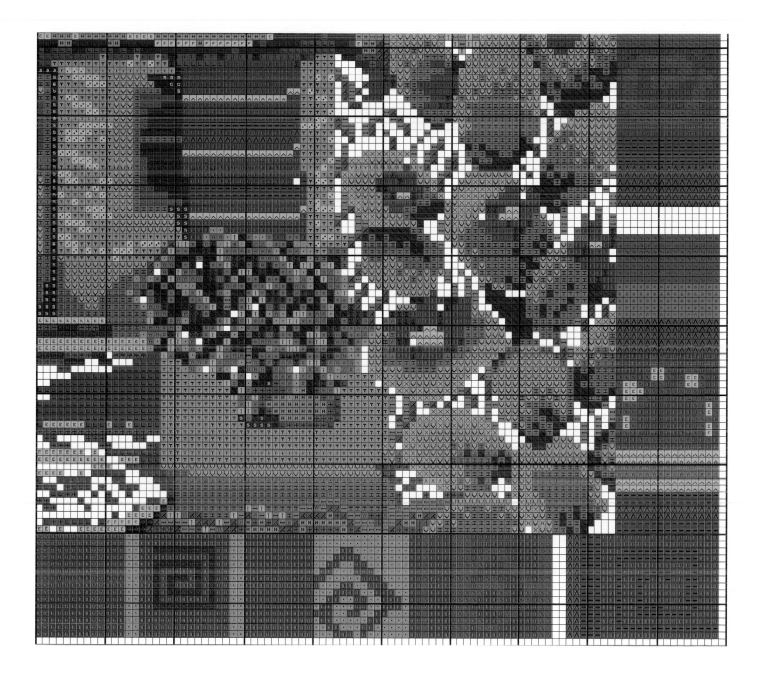

Honeysuckle Village

The design for Honeysuckle Village
came from images stored in my
mind from the villages I have lived
in or visited throughout my life.
As a child I lived in the English
counties of Somerset and Devon for
some years; later on I lived in the
Cotswolds, beautiful rolling rural
hills in south-west England.
Pretty villages such as Dunster,
Selworthy, Bourton-on-the-Water
and the cottages in the hamlet
where I lived near Cirencester, were
all instrumental in the forming
of this design.

RIGHT *This design makes a wonderful footstool
but such a lovely scene, almost a chocolate-box
image, would also look perfect mounted as a
framed picture.*

It was a pleasant task looking through old sketchbooks for watercolours of cottages as well as old photographs in order to find the right inspirational references for this design. Thatched cottages like these were part of my childhood memories from the time that I lived in Somerset and rode through the villages. These still boasted many carefully tended thatched roofs on the old cottages.

As a girl I was horse-mad and eventually my parents realized that I was serious about having a pony of my own. In those days, in the rural communities of Exmoor, owning a pony was not expensive, so I was lucky enough to spend all my spare time riding through the deer park at Dunster and over the wide, open expanses of Exmoor. This gave me an incredible amount of freedom and my hours were spent exploring its villages and countryside. I rode over Grabist, which was part of the inspiration for the hymn 'All things bright and beautiful'. I loved riding over the old woolpack bridge at Dunster, which crosses the river Aville in such picturesque fashion. Selworthy

was another favourite, a very small hamlet at the time, with an open stream running down beside the houses. We used to walk over North Hill from Minehead and along the ridge and down into Selworthy – the views were absolutely incredible. North Hill used to be covered in rhododendron flowers in the spring, along with lovely, fragrant gorse. Bourton-on-the-Water holds more recent memories of when my own children were young and played for hours in the shallow river that flows through the village. Lovely mellow Cotswold houses face the river which is edged by fresh lawns.

I have always planted honeysuckle in the garden of every house I have lived in, if it was not already there. I love the circular formation of the tubular flowers and the heavenly fragrance. It brings back memories of long walks down country lanes after a summer shower and the perfume of the rain-drenched honeysuckle which grew wild in the hedgerows. Honeysuckle Village is a nostalgic design for me and brought back many beautiful memories.

Honeysuckle Village

Design Size

30cm x 30cm (11¾in x 11¾in) approximately

Stitch Count

166 x 166

Materials

- 41cm x 41cm (16in x 16in) 14-count evenweave in blue (Fabric Flair NJ429.21.140)
- Size 24 or 26 tapestry needle
- Anchor stranded cotton (floss) as listed in the key

STITCHING GUIDELINES

This design can be stitched on any 14-count fabric such as Aida or linen, but I chose a very pretty blue evenweave which really brings the design to life and which looks very attractive mounted on a footstool.

I chose to begin this design by first stitching the honeysuckle flowers and foliage and then I had to be careful not to touch them too much while I was stitching the rest of the piece! So I suggest using the traditional approach of finding and marking the centre of the fabric (see Techniques page 99) and the centre of the chart (which is indicated by arrows), and stitching outwards from the centre.

The entire design is worked in whole cross stitches using two strands of Anchor stranded cotton (floss). There are many close shades and it is a good idea to sort out the colours and put them on a thread organizer before beginning to stitch.

The blue of the fabric suggests the water in the river and areas of the sky, so please use the colour suggested or one that is close in shade, otherwise the end result will be very different.

Once the stitching has been completed, remove any guidelines and steam iron gently on the back of the embroidery, placing it face down on a towel to avoid flattening the stitches. Then the design can be mounted as a footstool, as described in Making Up, page 102.

KEY
Anchor stranded cotton (floss)

- 66
- 68
- 92
- 145
- 146
- 226
- 241
- 244
- 246
- 255
- 256
- 295
- 302
- 306
- 369
- 386
- 387
- 392
- 878
- 886
- 888
- 895
- 898
- 904
- 905
- 945 *x2*
- 1002
- 1027

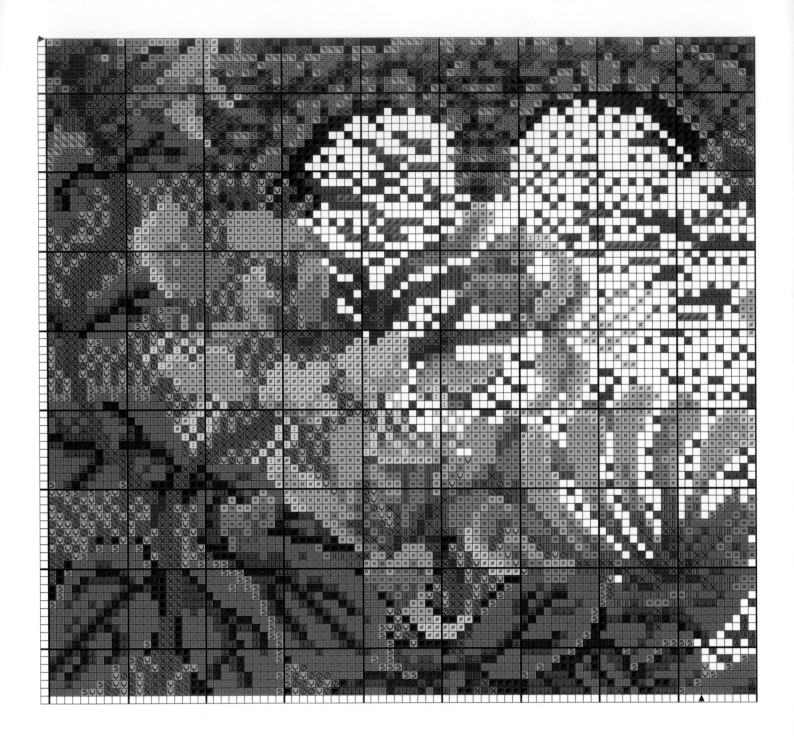

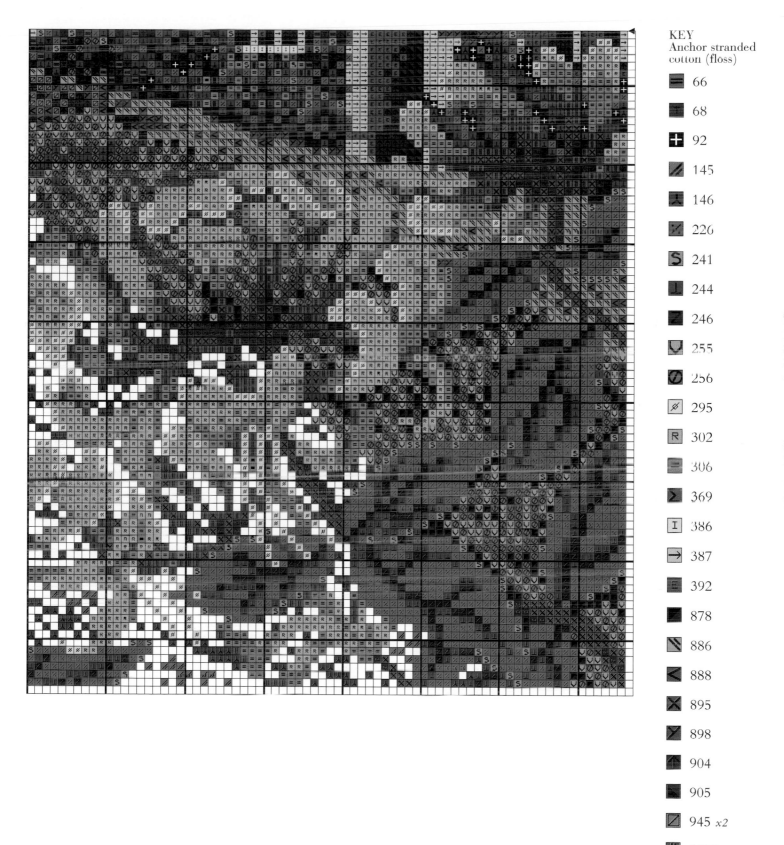

▬	66
▬	68
✚	92
◪	145
⊥	146
◪	226
S	241
⊥	244
▬	246
∪	255
∅	256
R	302
▤	306
▶	369
I	386
→	387
▤	392
■	878
◩	886
◀	888
✕	895
◪	898
◣	904
▬	905
◪	945 *x2*
▥	1002
▦	1027

Eilean Donan Castle

In 1220 Alexander II, King of Scotland, built a huge tower house on a tiny rocky island in order to combat Viking raiders who were threatening his shores. The builders sunk a well in the rock to a depth of 10m (32ft), an incredible feat of engineering. The name 'Eilean Donan' is Gaelic for 'Donan's island' – Donan being a 7th century saint who is thought to have lived the life of a hermit on this island.

RIGHT *I had great fun finding the fabrics that I felt would set this view of Eilean Donan castle off to greatest advantage. The design could equally well be made up into a large cushion or throw and would look wonderful in many different interiors.*

The origins of Eilean Donan go even further back than the 7th century; the remains of a Pictish fort were found in vitrified rock when the island was excavated, and opposite the castle is a sculptured impression in stone of a human foot. Similar sculptures have been found at the entrance to Iron Age settlements in other parts of Scotland.

The castle is such a beautiful building and set in the most inspiring landscape, it is unfortunate that it has had a turbulent and bloody history. Abbot Donan himself was said to have been killed here: '… and there came

Eilean Donan Castle

Design Size

37.5cm x 40cm (14¾in x 14⅞in) approximately

Stitch Count

207 x 208

Materials

• 48cm x 48cm (19in x 19in) 14-count Aida in teal green
(Zweigart No 626)

• Size 24 or 26 tapestry needle

• Anchor stranded cotton (floss) as listed in the key

STITCHING GUIDELINES

Begin by finding and marking the centre of the fabric
(see Techniques page 99). Many stitchers like to begin in
the centre of a design but this is a matter of preference.
I found this an exciting project to do. As it is quite
large, I decided to put all the flowers in before doing
anything more than outlining the view itself. I knew
that I would find it difficult to discipline myself to go
back to the flowers once I was absorbed in the castle
and its surroundings.

The entire design is worked in whole cross stitches
using two threads of Anchor stranded cotton (floss). It is
a good idea to sort the threads on to an organizer
before you begin stitching. It is important to buy the
shade of Aida fabric suggested, or a similar shade,
because the blue of the material suggests the water and
the sky in this design; therefore, if you use a different
colour, the end result will be quite different.

When the stitching is finished, remove any guidelines
and gently steam iron the embroidery on the wrong
side, taking care not to press too hard as this flattens the
stitches. It helps to place the design face down on a soft
towel before ironing. I have chosen to make this design
up into a wall hanging, a technique which is described
on page 103.

robbers of the sea on a certain time to the island when
he was celebrating mass. He requested of them not to
kill him until the mass was said, and they gave him this
respite; and he was afterwards beheaded and fifty-two of
his monks along with him.' (Martyrology of Donegal)

To counteract this imagery, there is an alternative
story relating to the origins of the castle's name. A local
legend tells of the King of the Otters, who was
distinguished by his coat of pure silver and white. He
made his home on the island and when he died he was
buried where the castle now stands. The Gaelic for otter
is *cu-donn* and this became donan over time. A much
more pleasant story!

My reasons for wanting to make this the subject of a
cross stitch design sprang from the magnificence of the
castle itself and the incredible beauty of its surroundings.
In spring, the hillsides abound with the bright pink of
rhododendrons, so I chose to frame the view with these
beautiful flowers. I also have fond memories of travelling
around Scotland and being so impressed by the beautiful
vast spaces, the clarity of the air and water.

Eilean Donan Castle 1

KEY
Anchor stranded
cotton (floss)

C	24
■	31 *x2*
I	33
◪	35
◢	59
V	167
◿	168
▲	169
T	245
Z	255
⌐	256
S	257 *x2*
◣	258 *x2*
II	265
�	266 *x2*
◩	267 *x2*
◐	269
↑	843
✕	888
⊟	896
K	898
U	904
A	945
9	956
Σ	8581

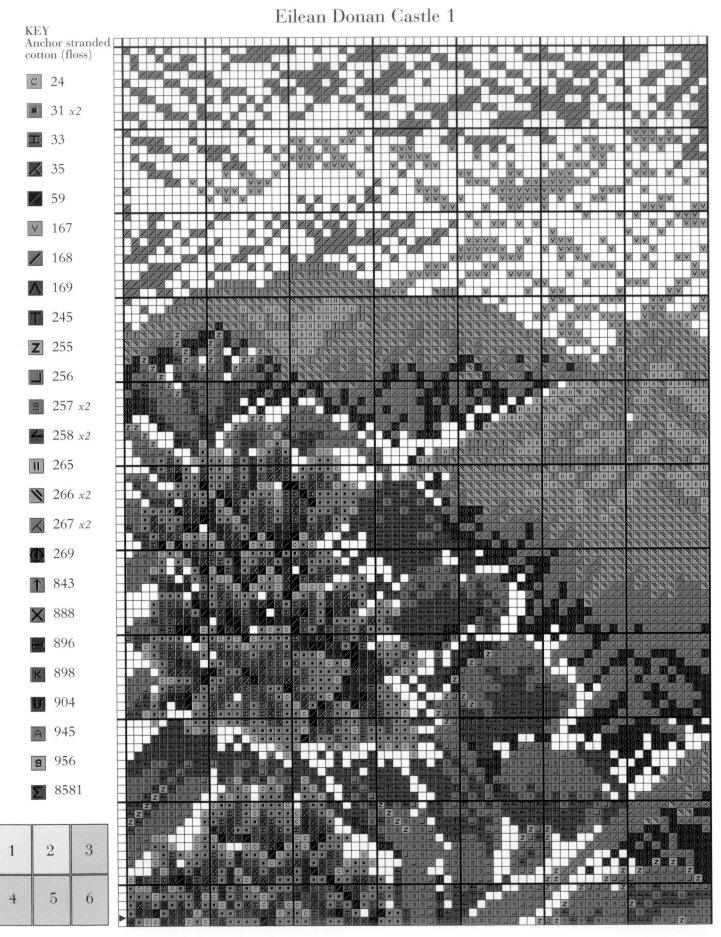

1	2	3
4	5	6

Eilean Donan Castle 2

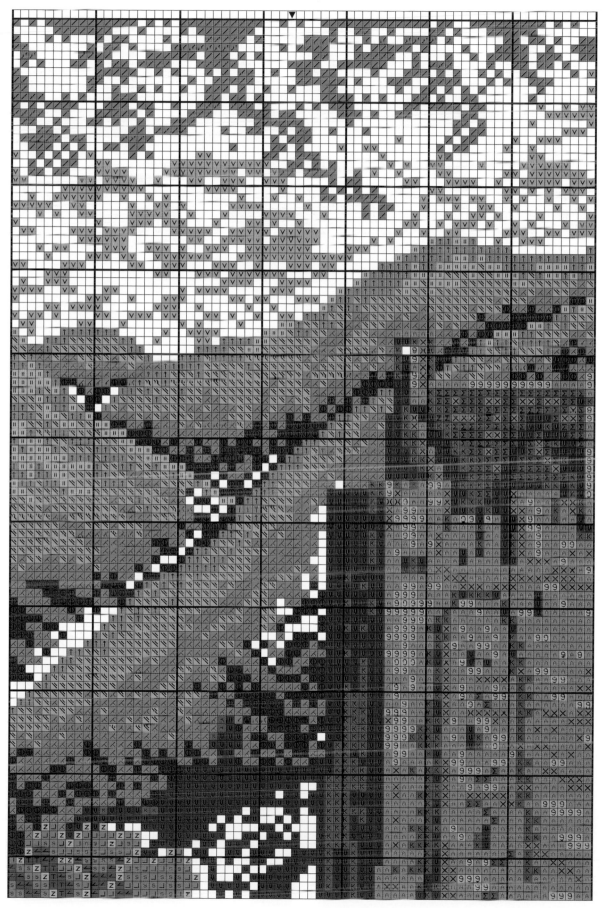

Eilean Donan Castle 3

KEY
Anchor stranded
cotton (floss)

C	24
■	31 *x2*
I	33
✕	35
◣	59
V	167
╱	168
∧	169
T	245
Z	255
⌐	256
S	257 *x2*
◢	258 *x2*
II	265
⦥	266 *x2*
✕	267 *x2*
◖	269
↑	843
✕	888
▬	896
K	898
U	904
A	945
9	956
Σ	8581

1	2	3
4	5	6

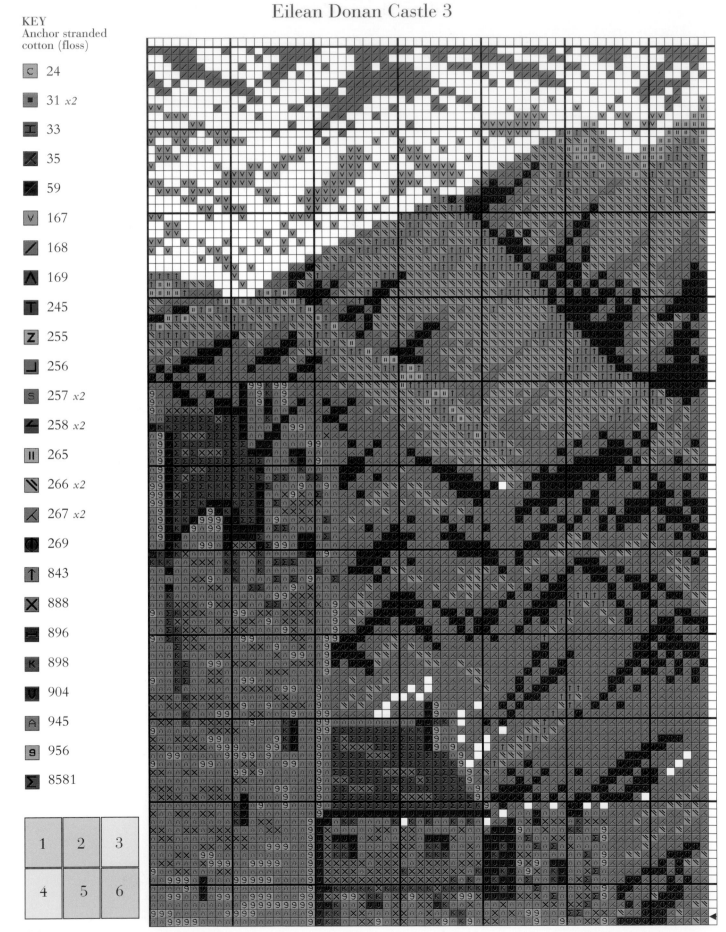

Eilean Donan Castle 4

Eilean Donan Castle 5

Anchor stranded
cotton (floss)

C	24
■	31 *x2*
⊥	33
◪	35
◣	59
V	167
◢	168
⋀	169
T	245
Z	255
⌐	256
S	257 *x2*
◣	258 *x2*
‖	265
◥	266 *x2*
◩	267 *x2*
◖	269
↑	843
X	888
⊟	896
K	898
U	904
A	945
9	956
Σ	8581

1	2	3
4	5	6

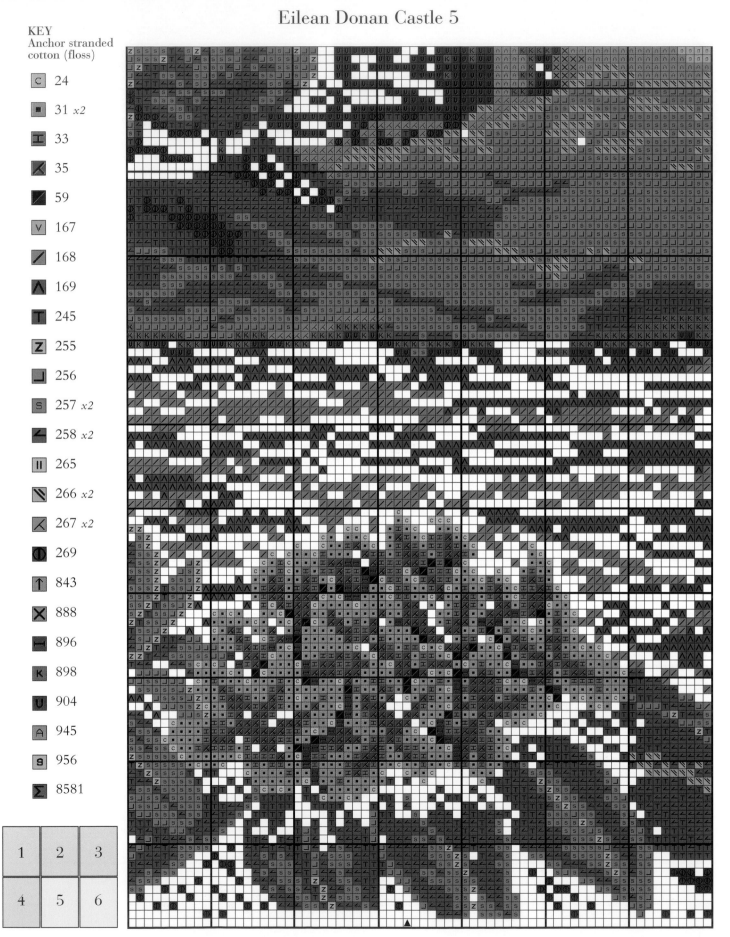

Eilean Donan Castle 6

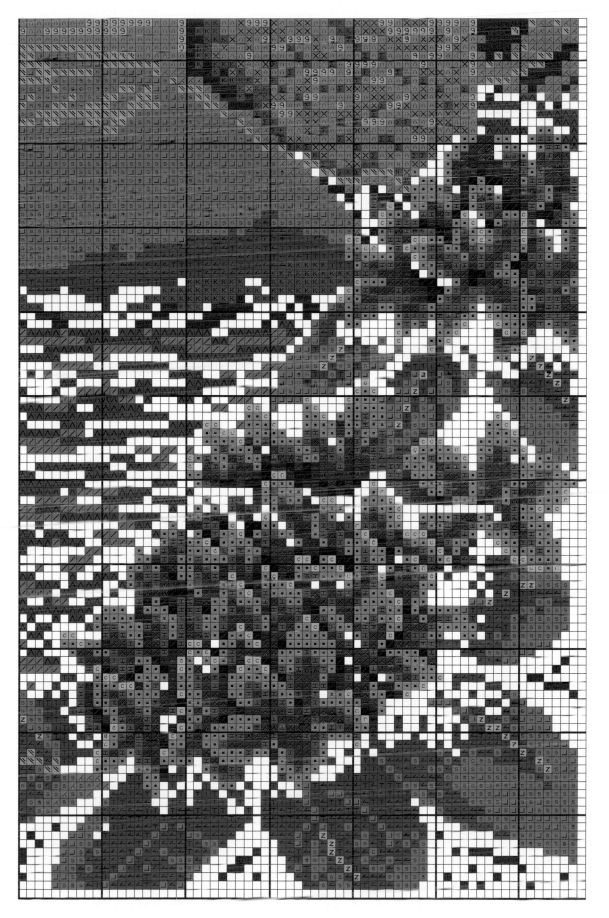

Italian House

This particular design was inspired by different Italian houses that captured my imagination whilst travelling through Italy. It is a particular 'flavour' that Mediterranean houses have, of sun-baked creamy terracotta walls, flowers tumbling over garden walls, vines laden with grapes, fruit trees and always the glimpse of a stone-paved patio filled with pots of geraniums. It is also reminiscent of the houses in the former Yugoslavia where we lived close to Dubrovnik, which is full of Italian-style houses.

RIGHT *This warm and evocative design would make an attractive framed picture or cushion. It could also be mounted in a square tray to make a useful item for alfresco dining.*

In my travels, I saw many different types of architecture and many different ways of building into the landscape. In Israel, I was very taken with the way that the Palestinian villages were barely visible in the landscape. They are built into the hills and crevices between the hills with local stone or into the hillside itself using it for some or all of the walls. In Italy, I loved the hill-top villages and the way that the houses there are also built into the hillside and perch there in the most picturesque fashion. In the heat of the summer, sometimes the only features visible are the warm terracotta-tiled roofs glistening in the sun, the rest of the buildings merged into the landscape.

Gardens are not only an essential part of life in Italy

because they still provide a diversity of food but they are synonymous with the Italian love of life and sense of beauty. They also provide a wonderful space for eating outside and generally enjoying the fresh air and climate. Wherever there is space in a garden or on the patio, a trellis or pergola can be found to provide wisteria, bougainvillea and honeysuckle with a climbing frame and the mixture of colour and perfume on summer days and evenings is exquisite.

Working on this design brought back a wealth of memories from my days in the former Yugoslavia and provides a constant pleasant reminder now that the picture is complete.

Italian House

Design Size

25cm x 25cm (10in x 10in)

Stitch Count

138 x 139

Materials

- 35.5cm x 35.5cm (14in x 14in) 14-count Aida in rich cream (Coats 0700)

- Size 24 or 26 tapestry needle

- Anchor stranded cotton (floss) as listed in the key

STITCHING GUIDELINES

The rich cream of the Aida fabric is used to suggest the sandy soil of the vineyard behind the house and the lighter tones of the stone flags of the patio, so it is important to use this colour or one that is similar in shade otherwise the end result will look different.

The entire design is worked in whole cross stitches using two strands of Anchor stranded cotton (floss). I suggest marking the centre of the fabric (see Techniques page 99) and design and begin stitching in the middle and working outwards. Having said that I have to admit

that I stitched the house first and then the fruit trees! As many of the colours used in this design are close in shade, it is a good idea to sort the threads on to an organizer before beginning to stitch.

When the stitching is completed, remove any guidelines and steam iron gently on the reverse side, with the front of the design face down on a soft towel in order to avoid flattening the stitches. The design can then be made up into a picture or a cushion or any appropriate item (see Making Up page 101).

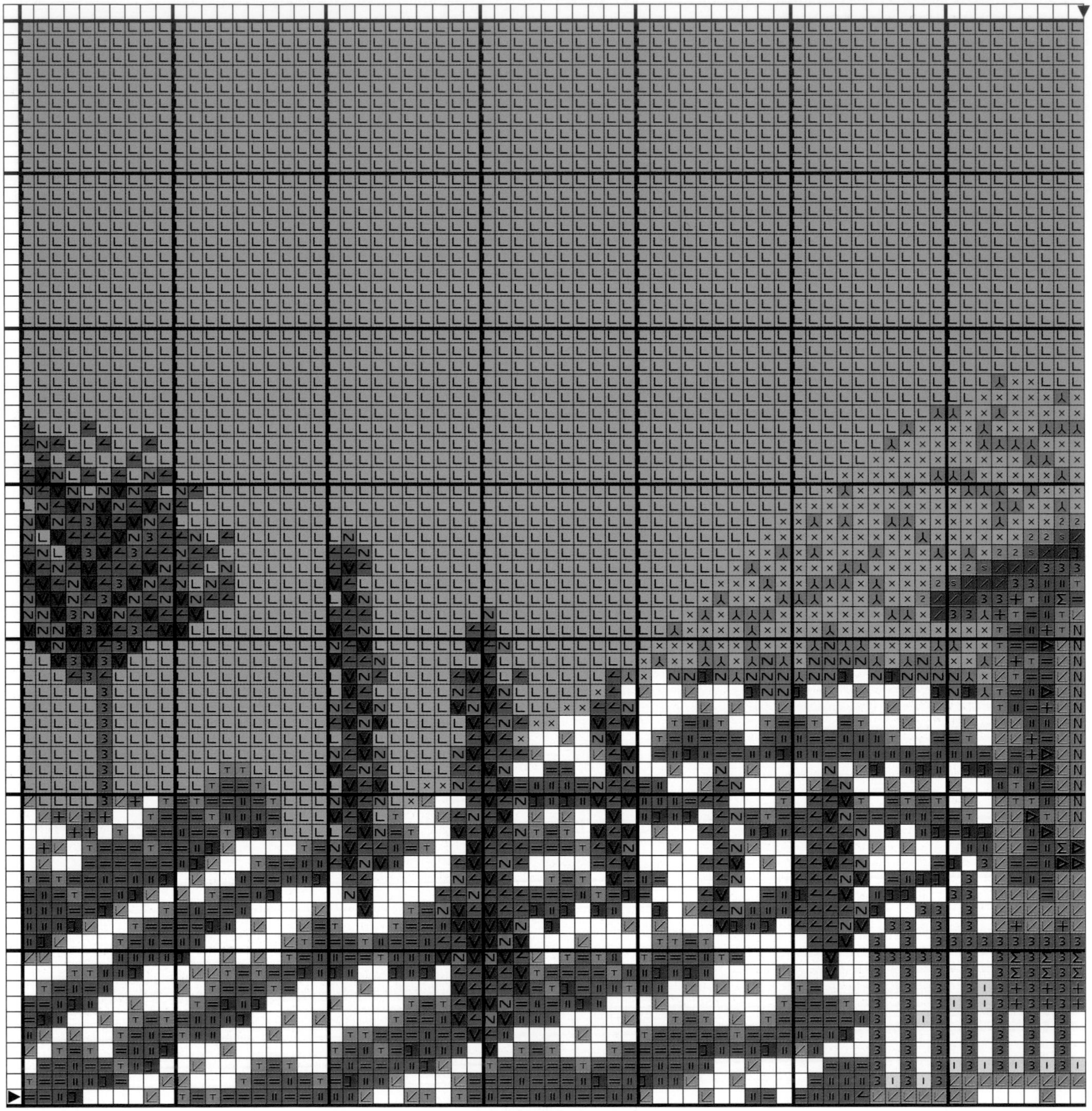

KEY
Anchor stranded
cotton (floss)

Symbol	No.	Symbol	No.	Symbol	No.	Symbol	No.	Symbol	No.	Symbol	No.	Symbol	No.
▼	11	L	167 *x2*	⅄	242	‖	258	I	325	∠	882	I	925
✕	13	N	168	N	244	⊥	268	s	337	+	883	2	1003
·	31	◤	210	T	255	╲	304	Σ	338	3	903	╱	1004
◀	40	×	241	=	256	z	324	V	878	◀	922	▶	5975

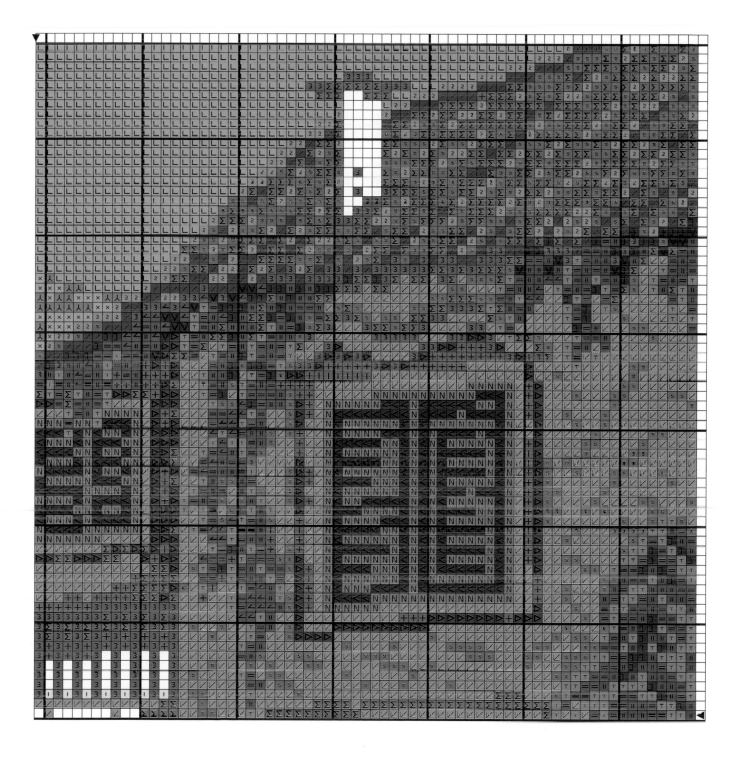

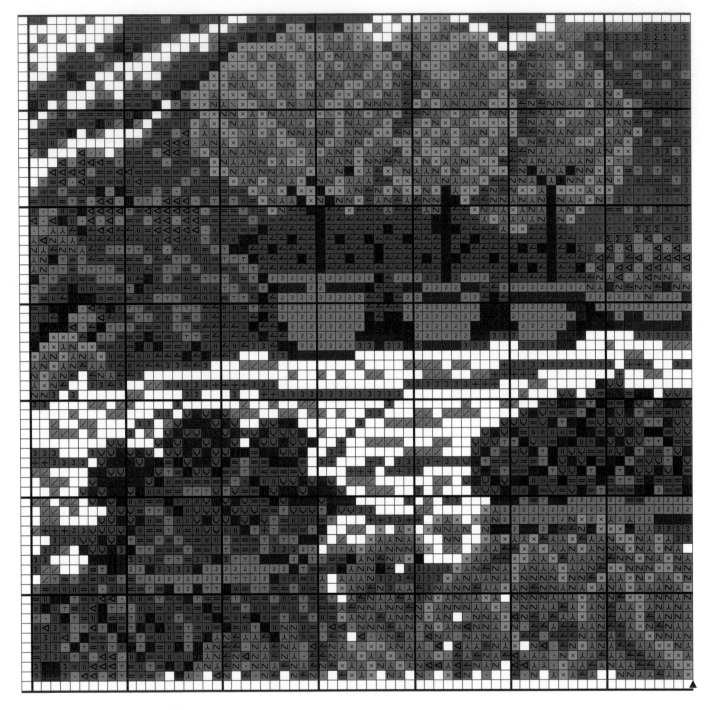

KEY
Anchor stranded
cotton (floss)

⋁ 11	∟ 167 *x2*	人 242	‖ 258	⊥ 325	∠ 882	Ι 925
✕ 13	N 168	N 244	▌ 268	s 337	✚ 883	2 1003
∙ 31	◢ 210	T 255	Σ 338	z 324	3 903	1004
◁ 40	✕ 241	= 256	⋁ 878	Σ 338	922	▷ 5975

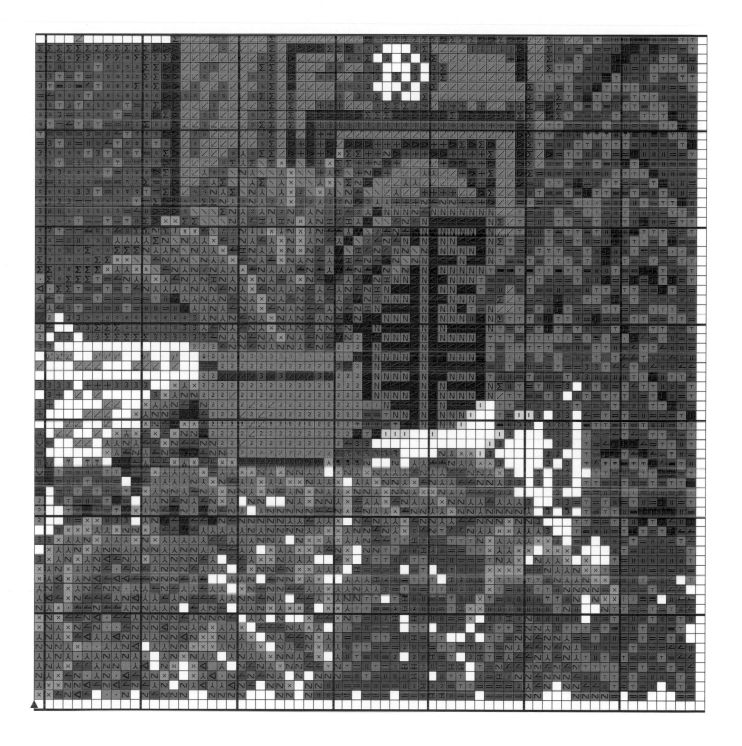

The Lighthouse

This lighthouse was loosely based on the Portland Head Light at Cape Elizabeth in Maine, USA. The beautiful coastline is adjacent to the Fort Williams Park, 90 acres (36 hectares) of exceptional walking country and ocean views. The lighthouse was built in the mid 1700s, principally to warn against British attacks. There was a keeper's cottage and other buildings around the light whereas other lighthouses had living accommodation within the lighthouse itself.

LEFT *This design is a versatile one and thanks to its subtle colouring would look attractive in different rooms, made up into a variety of objects – a picture, cushion, wall hanging or screen.*

Lighthouses originated more than two thousand years ago – the first record of a lighthouse is one that was built *circa* 299–200BC for the Pharaohs at Alexandria. Ancient lighthouses were often just a tower with a basket on top in which a fire could be lit. Later, candles were used. From 1760 onwards lighthouses were powered by various means including oil, early electric lights, petroleum-vapour lamps and gas, but it was not until electricity became a more dependable form of energy that electrical filament lamps became the norm. The automation of lighthouses in the UK began in 1910. This programme, completed in 1998, meant that lighthouses and light vessels could be controlled and monitored remotely either by a telephone line or by radio and therefore keepers did not have to live in them anymore.

I grew up by the sea and even though we moved many times, the places we lived in were always on the coast. The lighthouse at Beachy Head in Sussex, Britain is an early childhood memory and lighthouses have always fascinated me with their very different and isolated way of life. To be, in some cases, completely surrounded by massive seas with very little between oneself and the elements, seems to me to be a very brave and challenging form of existence.

With the shells in the foreground, the rocky cliffs and a blue sky, this design was a pleasure to create and stitch.

The Lighthouse

Design Size

26.5cm x 28cm (10½in x 11in)

Stitch Count

147 x 154

Materials

• 37cm x 38cm (14½in x 15in) 14-count Aida in sky blue (Fabric Flair N14.503)

• Size 24 or 26 tapestry needle

• Anchor stranded cotton (floss) as listed in the key

STITCHING GUIDELINES

In this design the blue of the Aida fabric is used as part of the sky, and in the sea and the shells and so it is important to use this colour or one very close in shade, in order to obtain the same finished result.

I found it fun to design and work the lighthouse first and provided that you centre the design carefully before you begin and mark the perimeters, you can begin wherever you like. In general it is a good principle to work downwards or outwards from the centre, to keep the stitching clean as your hands move over it. The shells were great fun to do and add an interesting foreground to the design both visually and in terms of stitching.

Only whole cross stitches are used in this design, with two strands of Anchor stranded cotton (floss) used

throughout. I used many shades that are very close in order to achieve subtle shadows; so it's a good idea to sort the threads on to an organizer before beginning.

Once the stitching is complete, remove any guidelines and carefully press with the right side face down on a towel so that the stitches are not flattened by the pressing. The design is now ready for making up – see page 101 for ideas.

KEY
Anchor stranded cotton (floss)

· 1	◹ 203	◥ 244	≡ 376	ℓ 852	⋂ 881	■ 1019	▲ 1041		
h 2	■ 211	+ 274	▯ 399	Z 853	✕ 939	w 1037x2	U 1045		
◥ 175	⋎ 225	⊤ 337	◢ 400	▲ 860	▷ 945	∿ 1038x2	◆ 5975		
■ 176	N 235	◺ 342	⊢ 842x2	◤ 871	f 1009	ε 1040	◺ 9575		

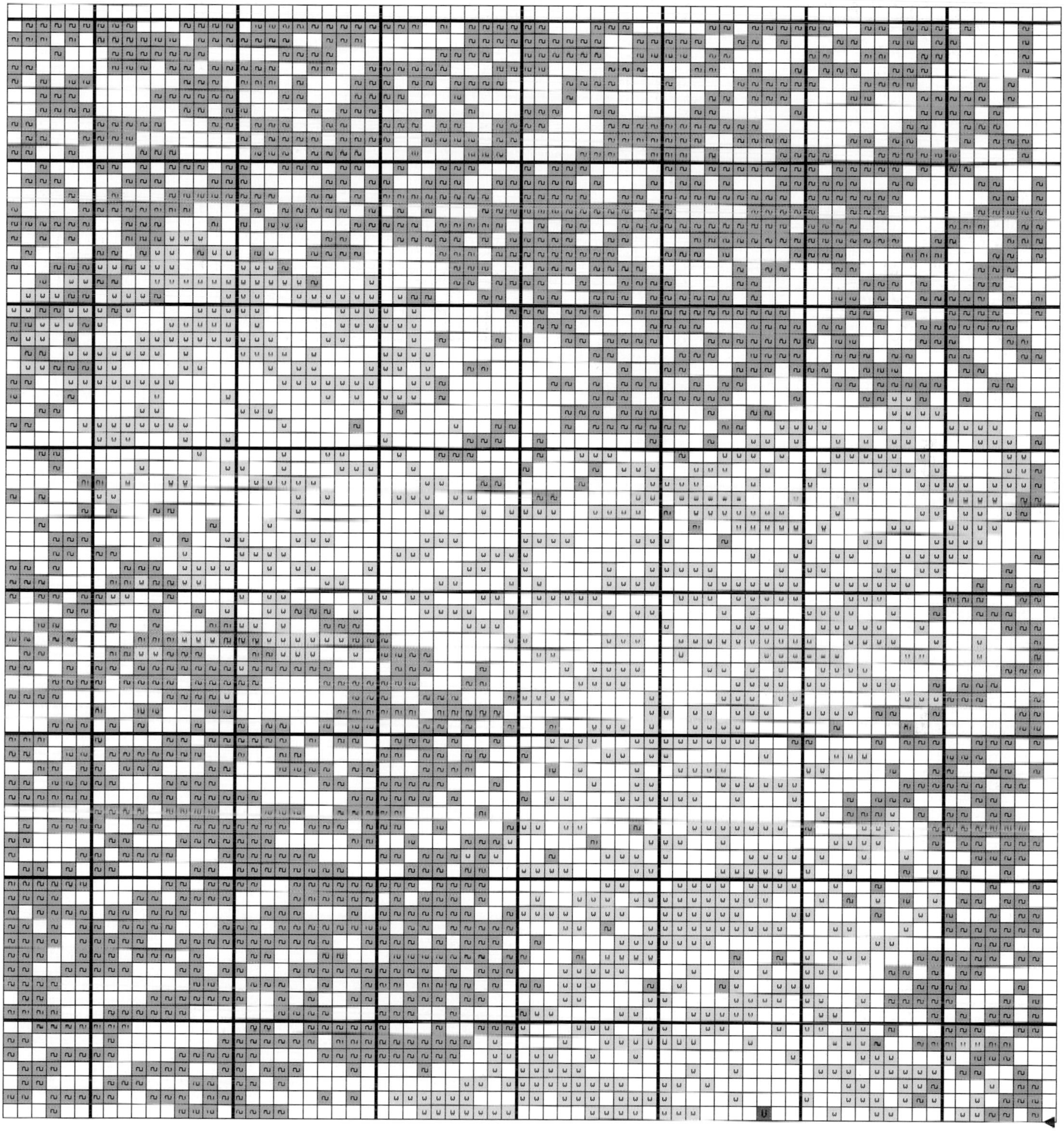

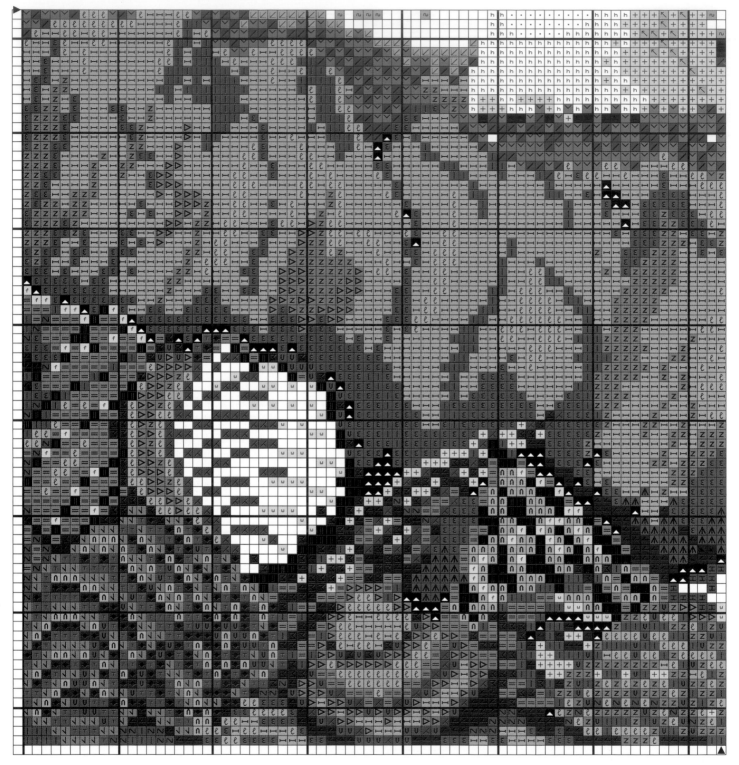

KEY
Anchor stranded
cotton (floss)

· 1	⚄ 203	⁄ 244	= 376	ℓ 852	⋂ 881	⊞ 1019	▲ 1041
h 2	■ 211	+ 274	∣ 399	Z 853	⤬ 939	⍵ 1037 *x2*	U 1045
⟍ 175	∨ 225	T 337	■ 400	▲ 860	▷ 945	∾ 1038 *x2*	◥ 5975
Ⓘ 176	⋉ 235	⟍ 342	⊢ 842 *x2*	◣ 871	f 1009	Ɛ 1040	⩘ 9575

Woodcutter's Cottage

The idea for this design came from a walk in the woods on the way to Wales. There was a sprinkling of snow and the woods were absolutely magical. On a well-worn path was an unexpected and delightful cottage in a clearing. It did not appear to be as lived in as the cottage in my design but the image stayed in my mind and leapt to the fore when I was thinking of different designs for this book.

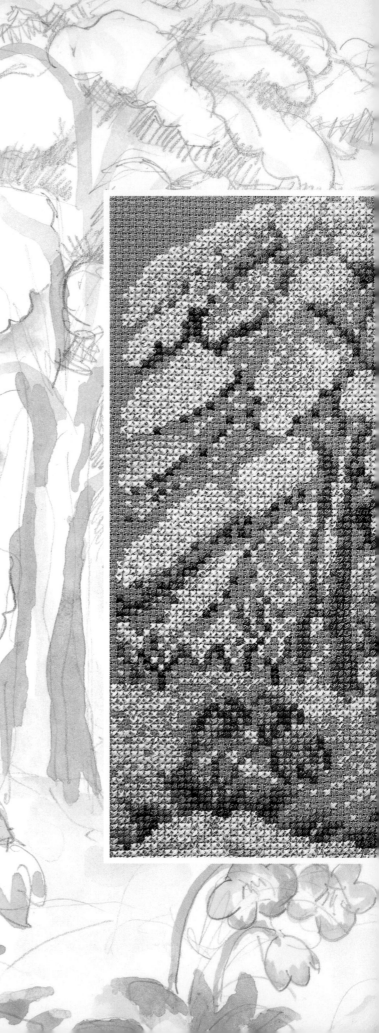

RIGHT *This delightful snowy scene would make a lovely framed picture but could also be made up as a Yuletide table runner by the addition of suitably festive framing fabrics.*

The hellebores in the picture, also known as Christmas roses, are partially artistic licence. Hellebores do grow in the woods in Wales but they are not this particular variety (*Helleborus atrorubens*), a pretty plum-purple with golden anthers. Sadly, even the native varieties are now considered rare: the woods used to be full of them when I was younger but now they are mostly found in gardens and are wonderful at brightening up the garden on dull winter days.

As this picture could have looked very 'white', I used the fabric colour to add depth and shadow. I also enjoyed myself playing with some very beautiful metallic threads, which sparkle just like snow does when certain lights fall upon it. This seemed to me to be the perfect stitching for those frosty winter days when all you wish to do is to sit in front of a cosy warm fire!

Woodcutter's Cottage

Design Size

28cm x 18.5cm (11in x 7¼in)

Stitch Count

154 x 102

Materials

- 38cm x 29cm (15in x 11½in) 14-count Aida in raindance blue (Fabric Flair N14.778)
- Size 24 or 26 tapestry needle
- Anchor stranded cotton (floss) as listed in the key
- Anchor Marlitt thread 800 White Bright
- Kreinik Very Fine (#4) Braid: 093 Star Mauve, 094 Star Blue and 095 Starburst

STITCHING GUIDELINES

I wanted to keep this design as clean and fresh looking as possible but at the same time I wanted to see how the cottage looked before putting in all the scenery around it, so I stitched the cottage first and then worked downwards for the rest of the stitching so that I was not constantly rubbing the stitches already worked. I suggest that you find and mark the centre of the design (see Techniques page 99) and work outwards from there.

As there are many close shades used to achieve the subtlety of snow, it is a good idea to put the threads into a thread organizer in daylight before starting to stitch. The grey-blue fabric is used in the design to suggest shadow and to give depth, so please use this fabric or a similar shade otherwise the end result will be very different.

The design is worked in whole cross stitches using two strands of stranded cotton (floss) mixed, in places, with Kreinik and Marlitt threads. I have used three Kreinik metallic threads – which I love – to add sparkle to the snow and some bright white Marlitt for an added sheen. Wherever Kreinik threads are used, mix one thread of Kreinik with one thread of white Anchor stranded cotton (floss). Where Marlitt is indicated, use only one thread. Marlitt can be springy to use but it is much easier if you run the length through a clean damp sponge prior to using. Use two strands of stranded cotton (floss) throughout.

When the stitching is complete, remove any guidelines and steam iron gently on the back of the embroidery, with the right side face down on a towel to avoid flattening the stitches. The design can then be mounted as a picture (see Making Up page 102).

KEY
Anchor stranded cotton (floss)

▶	1003
◫	1084
▷	379
◢	77
■	66
V	892
3	871
~	1037
↑	1060
⬐	878
∩	210
◀	267
⌂	268
Y	244
S	256
Z	279
T	874
\	2
⬛	926
≡	900
N	8581
◆	400

Marlitt
| ✛ | 800 *x3* |

Kreinik
(see text)
⁄⁄	095
o	094
—	093

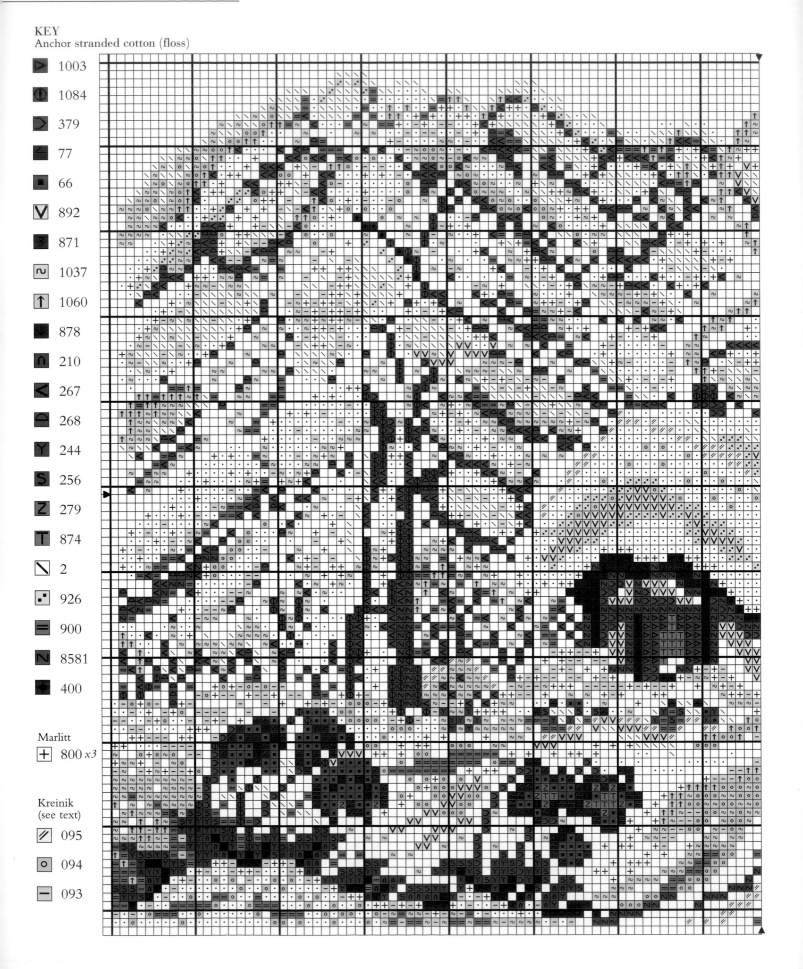

Castle of Dreams

My Castle of Dreams was based on Neuschwanstein Castle in Germany. This must be one of the best-known castles in the world, but I didn't realize this until after deciding to use it for this project. The seed of the idea for this design was planted when I saw a fairytale castle on the edge of Lake Bled in Slovenia. While looking for pictures of the lake, I came across Neuschwanstein Castle and fell in love with it. I later discovered that it had been the inspiration for the castle in Walt Disney's *Sleeping Beauty*.

RIGHT *This impressive design has been made up into a firescreen but would also look wonderful as a wall hanging or framed picture, or as a central panel in a big cushion.*

Neuschwanstein Castle, built between 1869 and 1886 as a royal palace in the Bavarian Alps, is the most famous of three palaces built for Louis II of Bavaria (1845–86). Not only is the castle magnificent with its turrets and fake medievalism but it is built in the most entrancing landscape; nearby are a massive 45m (146ft) waterfall and a beautiful bridge spanning a deep gorge. King Louis himself said about it, 'I intend to rebuild the old castle ruins of Hohenschwangau by the Pöllat Gorge in the genuine style of the old German knightly fortresses. . . the spot is one of the most beautiful that one could ever find'.

Although the castle has a wonderful dreamlike quality, the plans on which it was built were extremely practical and innovative and seemed almost revolutionary at the time. There was running water on all floors and a spring rising 200m (650ft) above the castle supplied it with excellent drinking water. There were lavatories on every floor, complete with automatic flushing, hot water for the kitchen and the baths, and a warm-air heating system to the entire castle. It not only looked beautiful but was comfortable as well — a combination not often found in castles!

It was quite a challenge attempting to retain the fairytale quality of the castle in cross stitch but I think it has succeeded really well and makes a rich and beautiful firescreen.

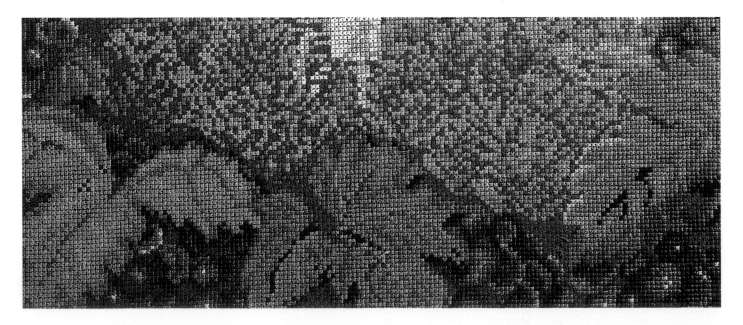

Castle of Dreams

Design Size

30.5cm x 36.5cm (12in x 15¼in)

Stitch Count

168 x 210

Materials

• 41cm x 48cm (16in x 19¼in)
14-count Aida in teal green
(Fabric Flair N14.626)
Important: if using for a firescreen,
measure the aperture and add
10cm (4in) to the fabric height and
width measurements and be sure to
centre the design on the fabric.

• Size 24 or 26 tapestry needle

• Anchor stranded cotton (floss) as
listed in the key

STITCHING GUIDELINES

The dark green colour of the Aida fabric is used as shadow and definition in many different parts of this design, so please be sure to use this colour or a very similar shade in order to achieve the same end result.

This design is quite complicated so I suggest finding and marking the centre of the fabric (see Techniques page 99) and working outwards from here. I stitched many different areas to make sure that the colours were working in the way I wished and this made it all very interesting. I particularly enjoyed designing the castle and watching it spring to life.

Only whole cross stitches are used in this design and it is worked using two strands of Anchor stranded cotton (floss) throughout. The rich colours of the grapes and vine leaves are quite close in shade as are many of the other colours used, so I suggest sorting all the threads on to an organizer before you begin.

Once the stitching is complete, remove any guidelines and gently steam press on the wrong side, right side down on a towel in order not to flatten the stitches. Make up as a firescreen following the instructions on page 102 or follow the firescreen supplier's instructions.

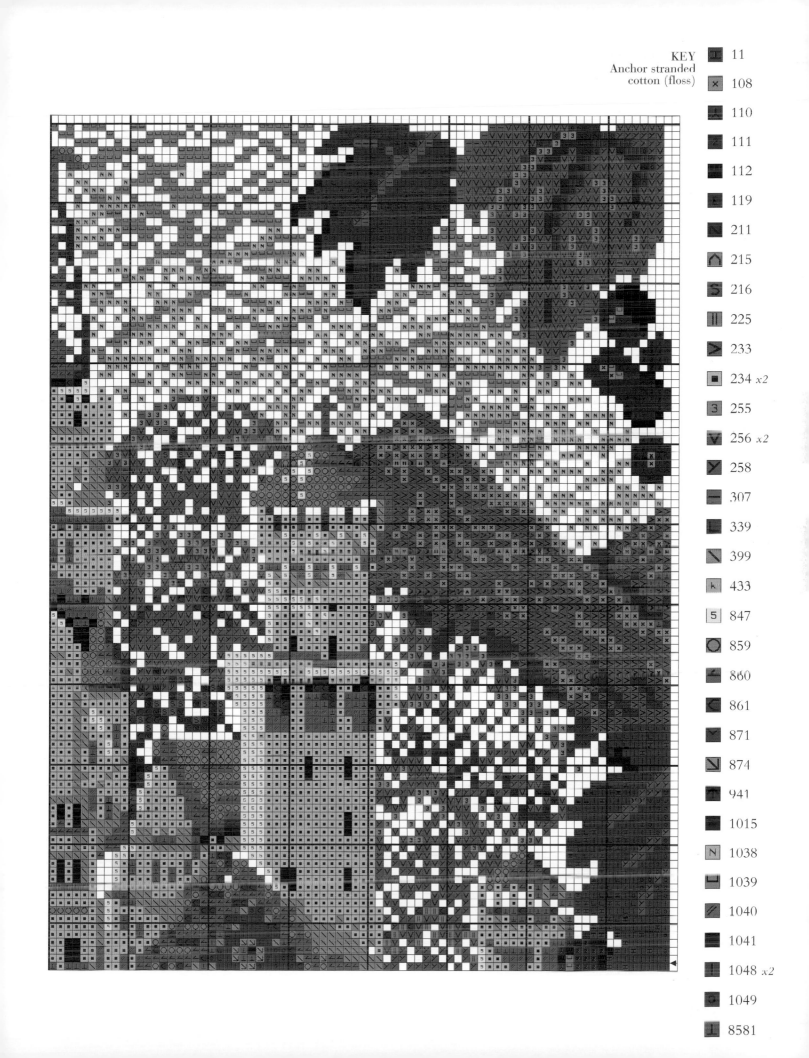

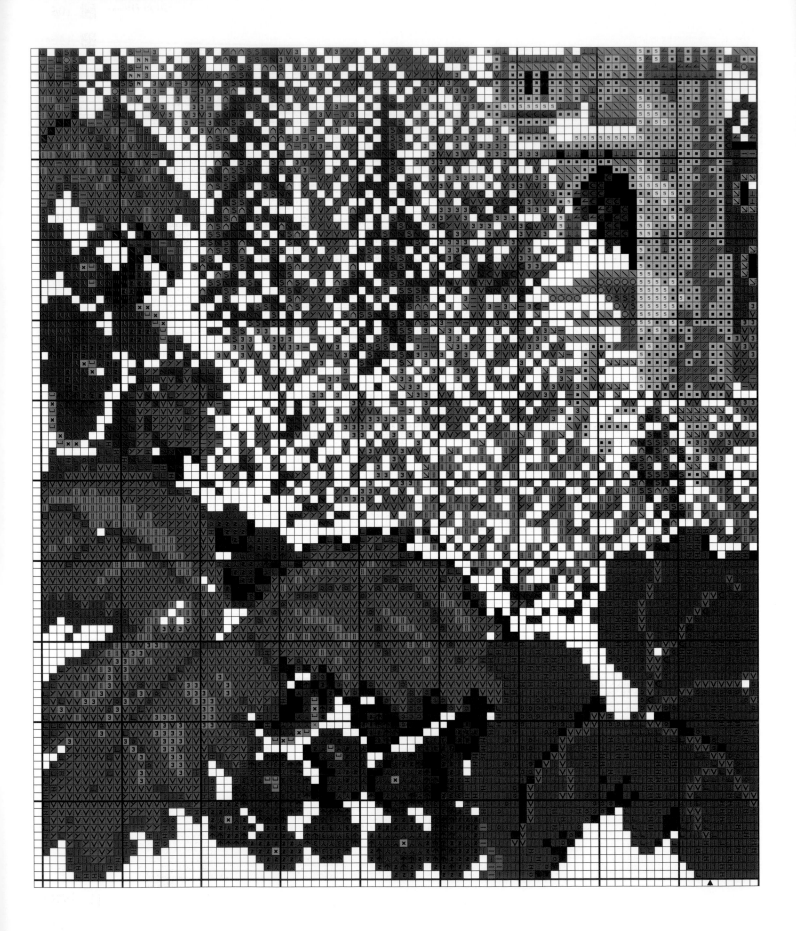

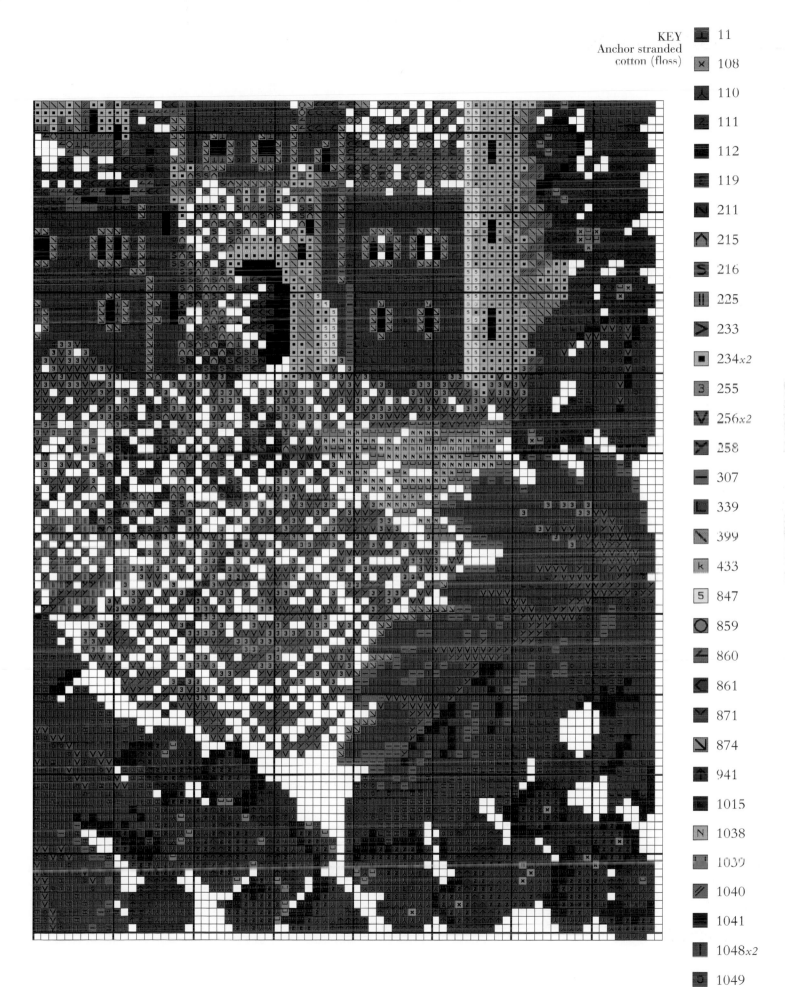

KEY
Anchor stranded cotton (floss)

Symbol	Anchor
┴	11
×	108
人	110
Z	111
■	112
Σ	119
N	211
∩	215
S	216
‖	225
>	233
▪	234x2
3	255
V	256x2
Y	258
–	307
L	339
╲	399
k	433
5	847
○	859
∠	860
<	861
⌄	871
↘	874
↑	941
▬	1015
N	1038
⊔	1039
//	1040
≡	1041
ǀ	1048x2
⊐	1049
⊥	8581

Chinese Pagoda

I have always thought of pagodas as being intrinsically Chinese but they were in fact introduced into China from India with Buddhism in the first centuries AD and are derived from Indian *stupas*, tombs honouring the dead. Several stone pagodas in China are still standing from that time. Early pagodas were simple, square structures but over the years evolved into much more elaborate buildings, both in shape and ornament.

LEFT *Such an elegant design as this would be perfect made up into a cushion, and would be even more sumptuous if a fabric border was added in one of the stronger colours from the design.*

By the 11th century, a distinctive type of pagoda was created in the Liao district of China, built in three separate stages – a base, a shaft and a crown, topped off by a spire. Pagodas were generally devoted to sacred usage and although often situated in gardens, were usually shrines rather than ornamental garden houses.

Widely speaking, the term pagoda is used to describe diminishing tiered roofing and is popular throughout Japan, Thailand, China and Nepal, where they are perhaps the most important and significant feature of the country's architecture. In a literal sense, it means structures that are made like pyramids and pagodas do indeed look like a stack of pyramids.

In China, up until the Communist regime, the development of religious thought and garden style went

Chinese Pagoda

Design Size

27.5cm x 26cm (11in x 10¼in)

Stitch Count

152 x 144

Materials

- 38cm x 36cm (15in x 14¼in) 14-count Aida in pale blue (Coats No 4600)
- Size 24 or 26 tapestry needle
- Anchor stranded cotton (floss) as listed in the key

STITCHING GUIDELINES

The colour of the fabric in this project is extremely important to the overall look of the design as the green is used throughout to suggest different aspects of the design, so please be sure to use the right colour or a very similar shade to obtain the same end result.

As there are many spaces in this design, I suggest marking the centre of the design and fabric (see Techniques page 99) and working outwards from that point. I thoroughly enjoyed designing this project as it is so different from anything that I have created previously. I was particularly pleased with the way the pagoda and the waterfall turned out. I used many close shades to convey subtlety and realism and it is a good idea to organize all the threads on a sorter before starting to stitch.

Only whole cross stitches are used in this design, with two strands of Anchor stranded cotton (floss) used throughout.

Once the stitching has been completed, remove any guidelines and steam iron gently on the back of the embroidery with the right side face down on a towel to avoid flattening the stitches. The design can then be mounted as a picture or made up into a cushion — see Making Up page 101.

hand in hand and the pavilion pagodas in gardens reflected this. Pagodas were built from various materials, mostly wood, stone and brick and several different types evolved over the centuries, such as dense-eaved pagodas with many layers, tower pagodas and pavilion pagodas. I have used a pavilion pagoda in this project. These were generally built of wood and exhibited truly extraordinary craftsmanship and carpentry.

The landscape around my pagoda is based on a Zen garden, originally a style of garden developed in the Zen monasteries, with deceptively simple arrangements of rocks, moss and gravel carefully positioned for the promotion of spiritual contemplation and calm. I have always been interested in Zen gardens and have drawn on photographs of these in this design. Beautiful fragrant almond and cherry blossoms frame the scene and the pagoda is built amongst the water gardens which is a favourite place for shrines.

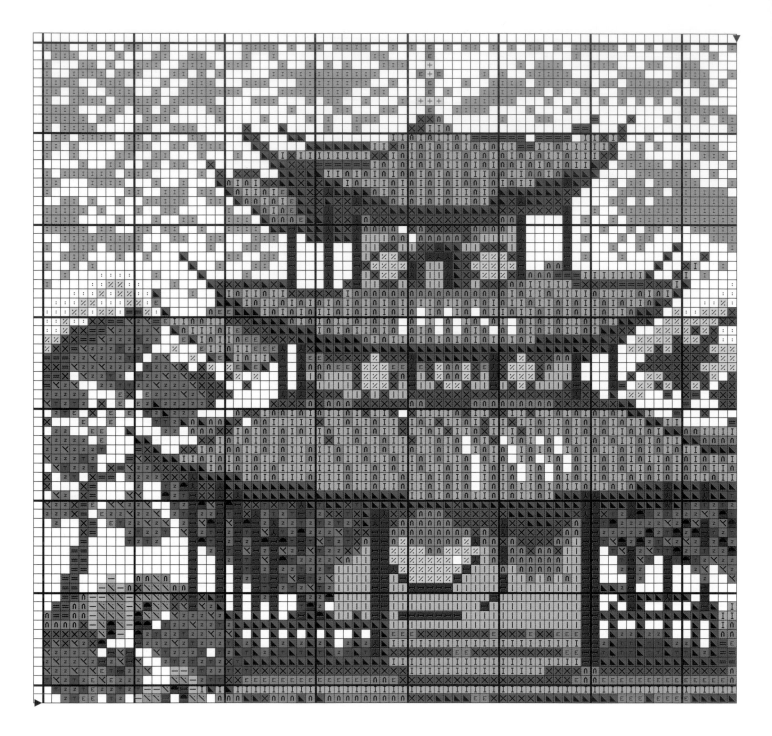

KEY
Anchor stranded
cotton (floss)

⠒ 2	I 167x2	⊤ 211	⁒ 274	I 376	═ 860
─ 49	╱ 168	⏛ 227	+ 279	I 842	◣ 1041
╲ 60	╳ 204	A 242	⊟ 338	∩ 853	╳ 8581
■ 68	z 209	C 244	⊿ 339	E 855	

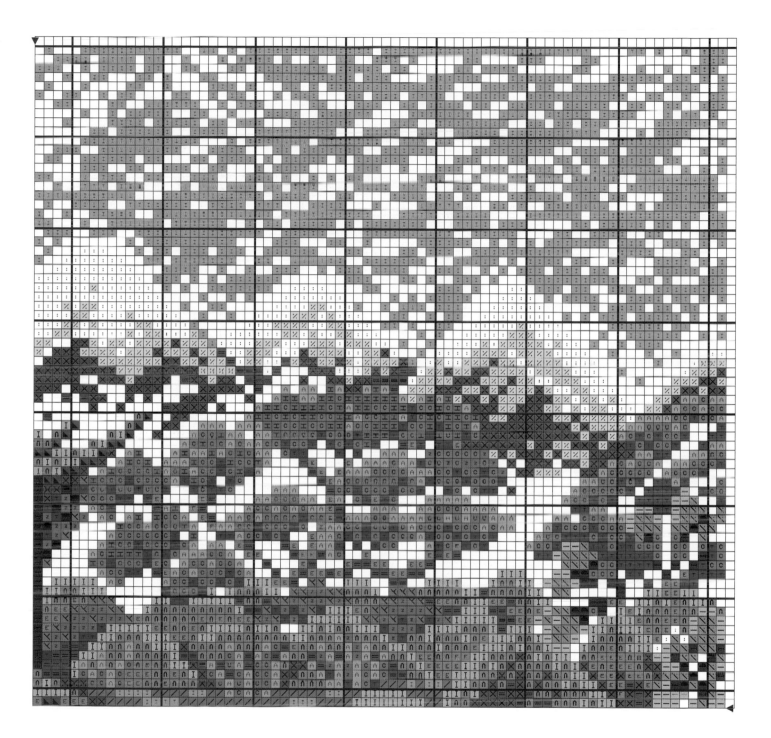

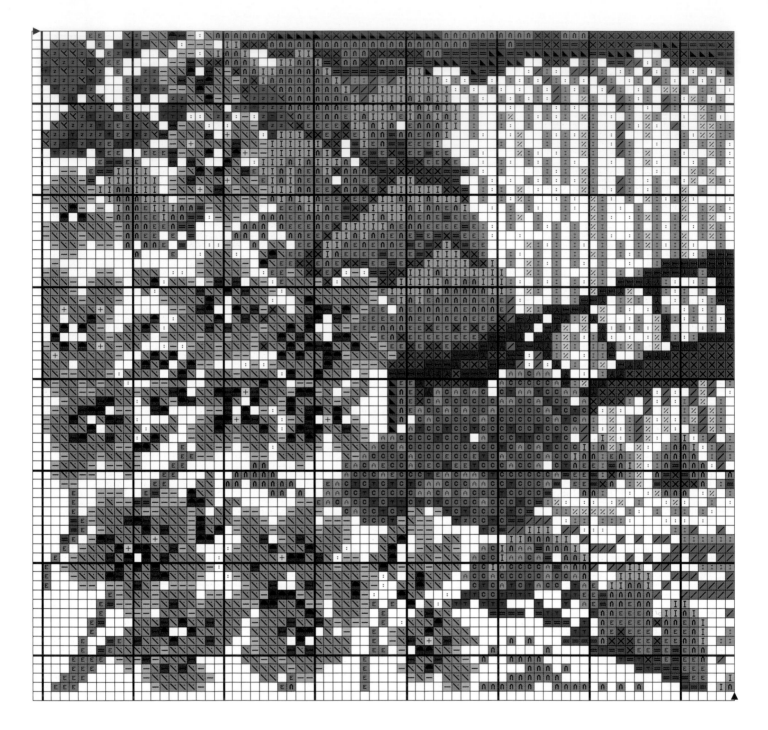

KEY
Anchor stranded
cotton (floss)

Symbol	No.	Symbol	No.	Symbol	No.	Symbol	No.	Symbol	No.
:	2	I	167x2	T	211	⁒	274	I	376	=	860
–	49	/	168	I	227	+	279	I	842	◣	1041
＼	60	＼	204	A	242	▬	338	∩	853	X	8581
■	68	z	209	C	244	▮	339	E	855		

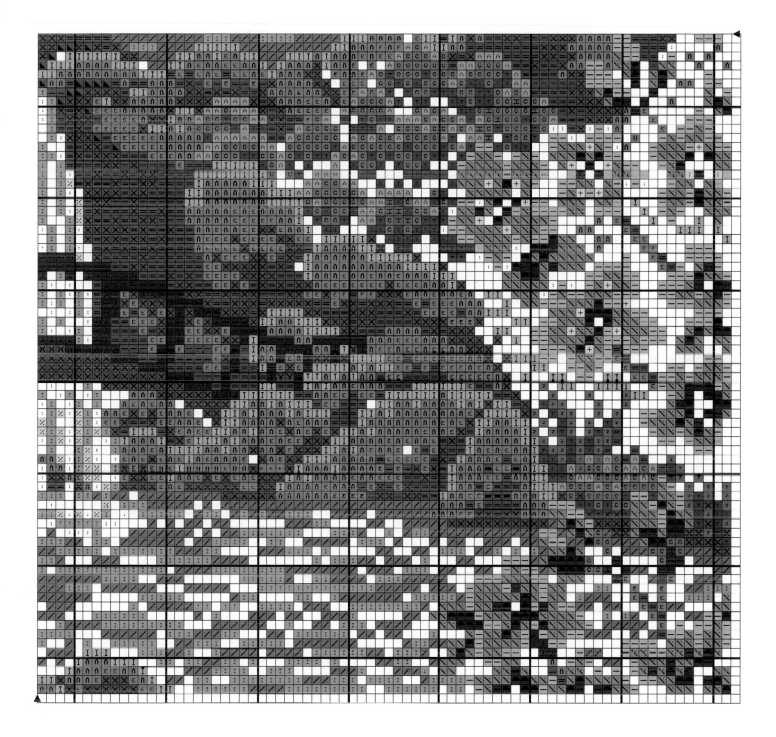

French Manor House

This design was based on an extraordinarily beautiful manor house in the area of France known as Pays d'Auge. It was built late in the 15th century and over the years has shifted with the terrain, so that it is now attractively curved and bent but still massively robust.

It has wonderful mullioned windows and although it wasn't possible to capture intricate detail in this design, the mellow tones of the brickwork and timber have been conveyed.

RIGHT *This wonderfully sunny design would make the perfect picture or cushion to remind you of summertime and holidays abroad.*

I have travelled through France several times and have marvelled at the wonderful manor houses that I have seen there, particularly in Normandy. Sunflowers add additional life and colour to this design although Normandy is better known for its apple orchards, green pastures and profusion of milk and cream. It is a region of abundance, with fertile lands and rich harvests from land and sea and has a wonderfully temperate climate where flowers bloom all year round.

The favourable climate and successful agriculture of Normandy has produced considerable affluence and this has resulted in hundreds of manor houses in the area, ranging from small and modest to very large and impressive. Some of the buildings are timber-framed, others are constructed in brick and stone, erected by dignitaries in bygone centuries to mark their success in a lasting way.

As you can see from the illustration on the right, I often start my designs as pencil or crayon sketches of the main feature, then I can superimpose a foreground

or background until I find one that really pleases me.

I would love to have been able to design other projects based on the interior of the house, which is exquisitely carved and painted. There are certainly many wonderful inspirations to be found in the buildings and landscape of the Pays d'Auge, which is also called, understandably, the heart of Normandy.

French Manor House

Design Size

22.5cm x 19.25cm (9in x 7⅝in)

Stitch Count

125 x 106

Materials

- 33cm x 30cm (13in x 11¾in) 14-count Aida in teal green (Fabric Flair N14.626)
- Size 24 or 26 tapestry needle
- Anchor stranded cotton (floss) as listed in the key

STITCHING GUIDELINES

This was a wonderfully cheerful design to create and stitch and although I was very keen to see the house completed, I had to keep going back to the sunflowers.

The teal green of the fabric is very important to the design as it is used extensively to suggest dark leaves and shadows, so be sure to use this colour or one very similar in shade in order to achieve the same result.

The design is stitched in whole cross stitches, with two strands of Anchor stranded cotton (floss). It is useful to mark the centre of the fabric (see Techniques page 99) whether you begin stitching from here or not, as it is a useful marker for counting. The colours used in many parts of the design are close in shade and it is a good idea to sort them on to a thread organizer before starting.

When the stitching is finished, remove any guidelines and gently steam iron on the back, face down on a soft towel to avoid flattening the stitches. The design is then ready to make into a picture or cushion or similar object – see Making Up page 101.

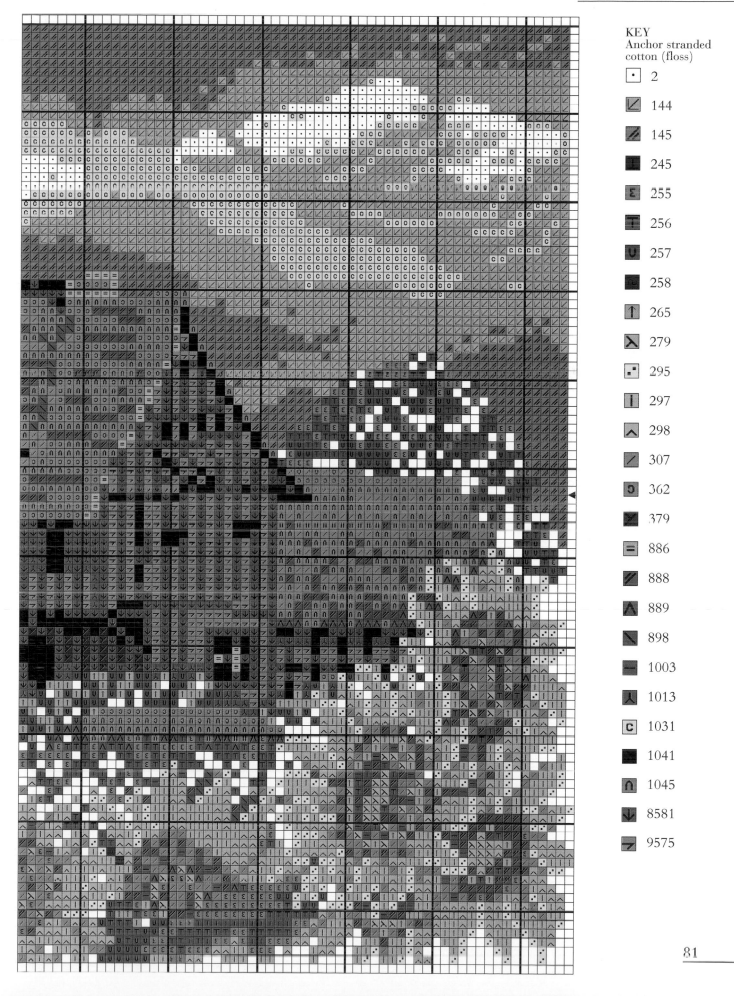

·	2
◹	144
◿	145
⊥	245
Ɛ	255
T	256
U	257
⊟	258
↑	265
✕	279
▪	295
I	297
∧	298
/	307
◓	362
⊻	379
=	886
◪	888
⋀	889
◥	898
⊜	1003
⅄	1013
c	1031
■	1041
∩	1045
↓	8581
↗	9575

Crofter's Cottage

This design was inspired by a visit to Scotland many years ago. As we drove around the lochs and the Highlands I remember being very impressed by a crofter's cottage in the most idyllic situation, surrounded by water, wild flowers and a little cottage garden with looming mountains behind it. Possibly not so idyllic in the winter time but in early summer it looked like paradise.

LEFT *This design would make a charming little wall hanging, especially if framed with suitable fabrics – see pages 101 and 103 for instructions.*

The Highlands of Scotland are deservedly famous for their rugged beauty but the land is also inhospitable and unsuitable for modern farming in the main part. Until recently there has been a steady decline in population although tourism is doing something to stem the flow and there have been many government measures to bolster crofting in particular.

Crofting, fishing and distilling have been the main occupations for centuries in the Highlands but fishing is now being threatened by diminishing fish stocks and crofting is a hard way of life due to the climate.

A croft, which has become almost synonymous with the word for the particular single storey whitewashed dwelling found here, is in fact a smallholding – a piece of land ranging in size from an acre (less than half a hectare) to over 50 acres (20 hectares) in some instances. The owner or the tenant of the land is known as a 'crofter'. Crofts were originally laid out in such a way as to provide a home and a food supply but few

are large enough now to provide an entire livelihood and larger more comfortable, but usually less picturesque, buildings have replaced many of the original dwellings.

I thoroughly enjoyed working on this evocative design and recapturing the glorious beauty of the Highland landscape.

Crofter's Cottage

Design Size
25cm x 25cm (9⅞in x 9⅞in)

Stitch Count
138 x 139

Materials

• 35.5cm x 35.5cm (14in x 14in) 14-count Aida in sky blue (Fabric Flair N14.503)

• Size 24 or 26 tapestry needle

• Anchor stranded cotton (floss) as listed in the key

STITCHING GUIDELINES

This design is stitched in whole cross stitches using two strands of Anchor stranded cotton (floss) throughout. The blue of the Aida fabric is used as part of the sky and the loch and it is important therefore to use this colour or a very similar shade in order that the finished piece looks the same.

The colours are very close in shade, particularly the flowers, so it is a good idea to sort all the threads on to an organizer before beginning to stitch. It is then possible to stitch in good artificial light as well as daylight, without getting the colours confused. It is useful to mark the centre of the fabric (see Techniques page 99) and the design even if you intend to start stitching from the side or top as it gives a useful reference point, particularly when there is a lot of dense stitching.

When the design has been completed, remove any guidelines and steam iron gently on the reverse with the right side face down on a towel to prevent flattening the stitches. The embroidery can then be made up into the item of your choice, such as a picture, a cushion or a little wall hanging (see Making Up page 101).

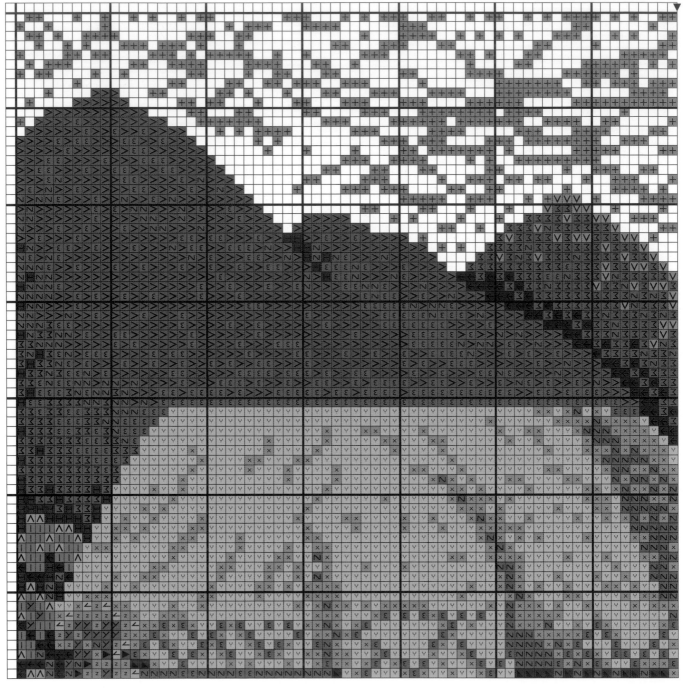

KEY
Anchor stranded
cotton (floss)

· 2	△ 76	Λ 225	z 255	∾ 305	⧎ 850	◼ 877	⊤ 1039
ⴺ 11	ⴹ 77	I 226	Y 256	·· 306	N 856	Y 886	Ɛ 1040
◣ 52	ⴹ 98	/ 241	∠ 265	∩ 391	> 870	⊨ 871	◼ 1041
■ 66	+ 145	▶ 246	∥ 304	V 849	⊢ 871	× 945	

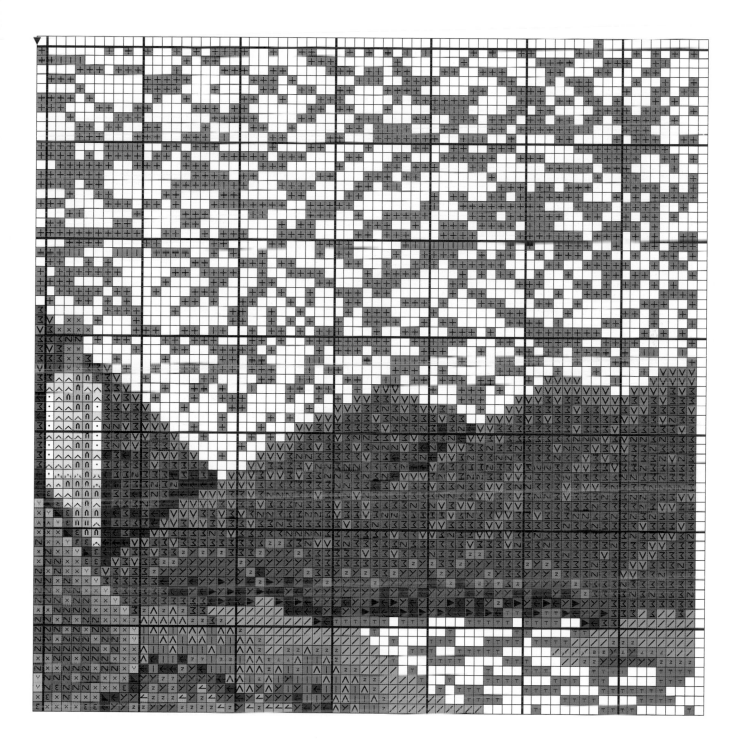

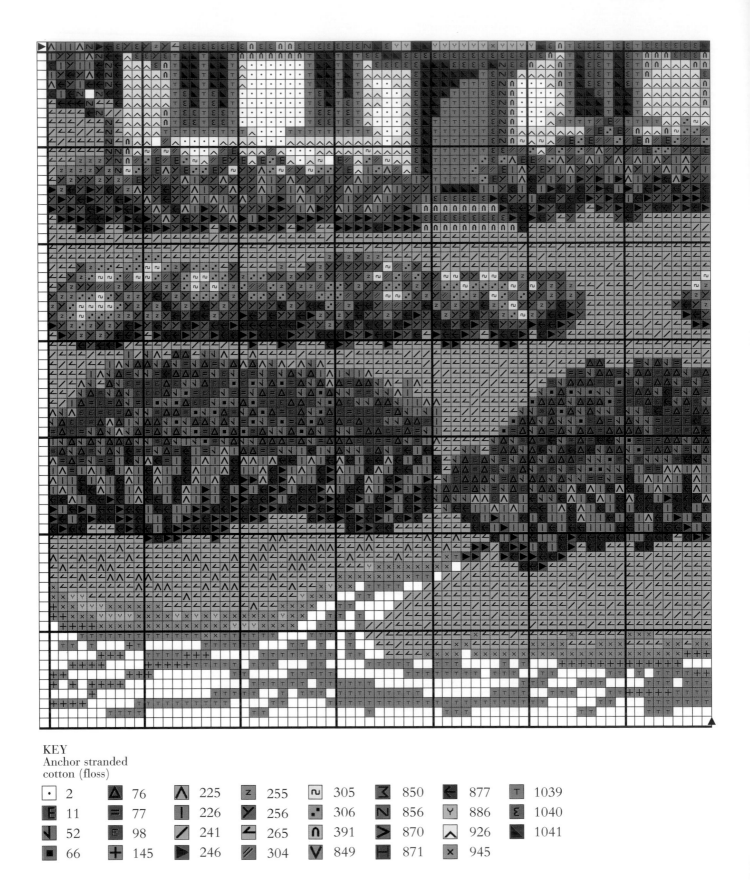

KEY
Anchor stranded
cotton (floss)

·	2	▲	76	∧	225	z	255	௹	305	◿	850	◀	877	T	1039
▤	11	═	77	I	226	⅄	256	·ᴵ	306	N	856	Y	886	ℇ	1040
◥	52	▣	98	╱	241	◢	265	∩	391	▶	870	∧	926	◣	1041
▪	66	➕	145	▶	246	⫽	304	V	849	⊦	871	×	945		

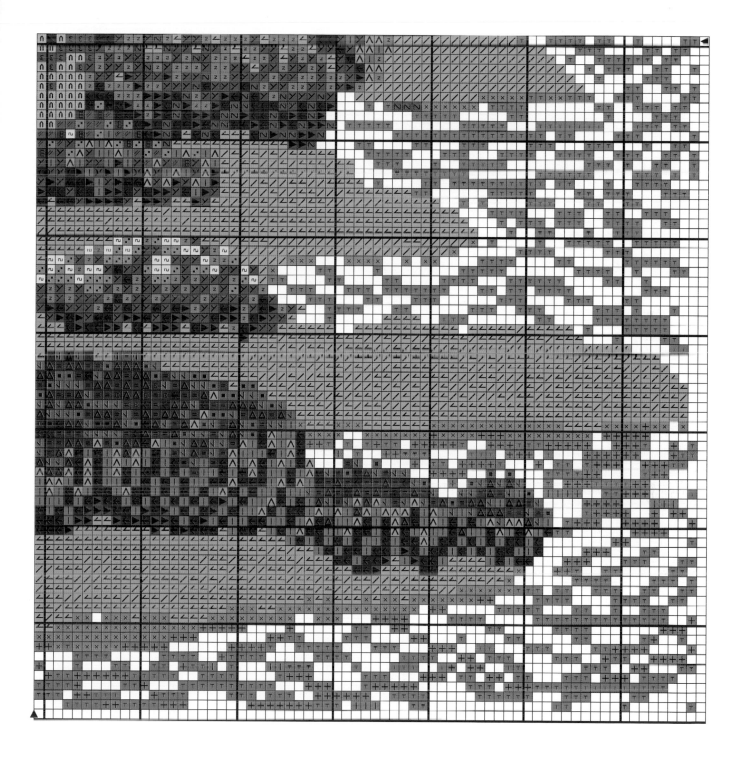

Venetian View

This design is a view of the Grand Canal in Venice from a window on the other side of this most famous water highway. This image comes from a memory of Venice when I was travelling across Europe some years ago. I think it was in Italy that I first noticed how beautiful geraniums are and what a glorious summer-long blaze of colour they give us, coupled with the pungent perfume of their leaves in the hot Mediterranean sun.

RIGHT *This Italian-inspired design would make a good companion to the Italian House on page 38, perhaps as a pair of pictures or two cushions to bring a touch of the Mediterranean to your home.*

Sometimes it seems strange to me that we take the magic of Venice so much for granted. When I was a child it seemed to be a dream come true – a city with waterways instead of roads! Venice has very few bridges but over the centuries that hasn't been a problem for Venetians, as the majority of traffic consisted of gondolas or small boats and the canals were more important than streets. Instead of bridges, the Venetians used *traghetti* (gondola ferries) – a cheap and convenient way of crossing the canals.

Venice comprises six districts known as *sestiere*, which are all self-contained with their own distinctive style and history. They have survived intact to this day mainly due to the fact that Venice is made up of numerous small

islands and the bridges and pavements were built principally to help people get around within a particular district, with longer distances always covered by boat.

It is not only the magic of the canals that makes Venice special but also the magnificence of the architecture; and the exterior views are only a foretaste of the incredible works of art and interior design that exist within many of the buildings on the Grand Canal. There are innumerable sources of inspiration for needlework in Venice and this design is only one of many that I would like to create from this truly beautiful place.

Venetian View

Design Size

25cm x 25cm (10in x 10in)

Stitch Count

139 x 139

Materials

• 35.5cm x 35.5cm (14in x 14in) 14-count Aida in ice blue (Coats 4600)

• Size 24 or 26 tapestry needle

• Anchor stranded cotton (floss) as listed in the key

STITCHING GUIDELINES

This design is worked in whole cross stitches, with French knots used for the people's hair. Two strands of Anchor stranded cotton (floss) are used throughout, but if you find this too bulky for the French knots, then use one strand and create more knots.

The pale blue fabric that I have used suggests the water, some of the paintwork on the houses and the sheen in the voile curtains, so it is therefore important to use the same colour or a very similar shade in order to achieve the same result. As some of the colours in this design are very similar in shade, it is useful to sort your

threads and put them on an organizer before starting.

The design is quite densely stitched and could be started at the top or bottom; it is still useful to mark the centre of the design and fabric even if you are not stitching from there (see Techniques page 99).

When the stitching is complete, remove any guidelines and press gently with a steam iron on the reverse, with the front side face down on a soft towel. This avoids flattening the stitches too much. The design can then be mounted and made up into a picture, tray insert or any other suitably sized object (see Making Up page 101).

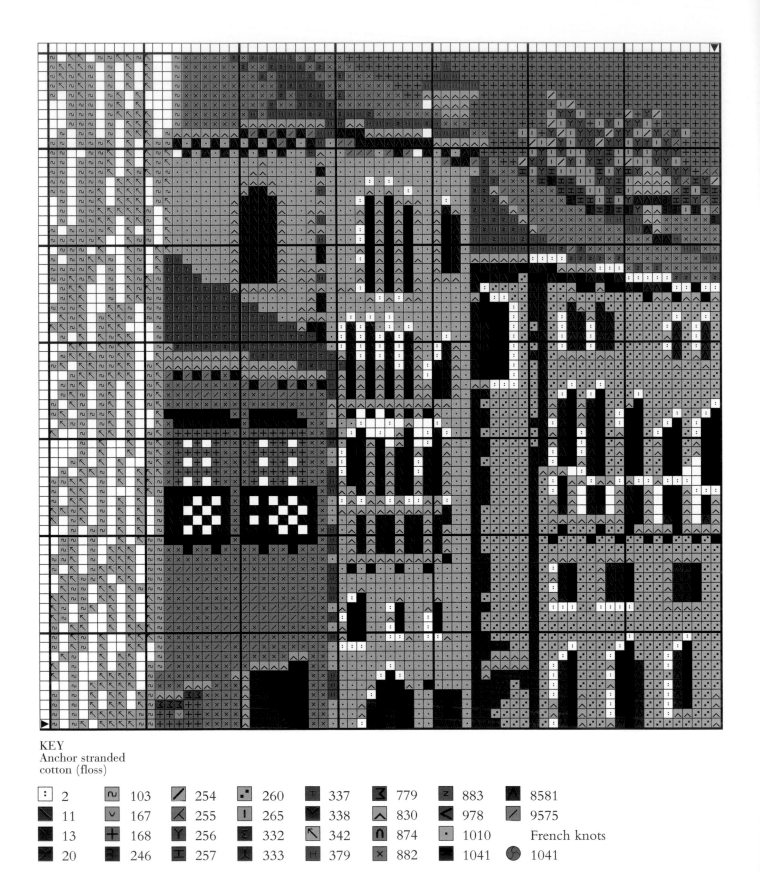

KEY
Anchor stranded
cotton (floss)

⊡ 2	℧ 103	╱ 254	▪ 260	⊤ 337	◣ 779	⊠ 883	◥ 8581
◥ 11	∨ 167	╳ 255	▮ 265	◢ 338	∧ 830	◀ 978	╱ 9575
◢ 13	✛ 168	Y 256	Σ 332	◥ 342	∩ 874	· 1010	French knots
◺ 20	▦ 246	⊥ 257	▦ 333	⊞ 379	✕ 882	◼ 1041	⊕ 1041

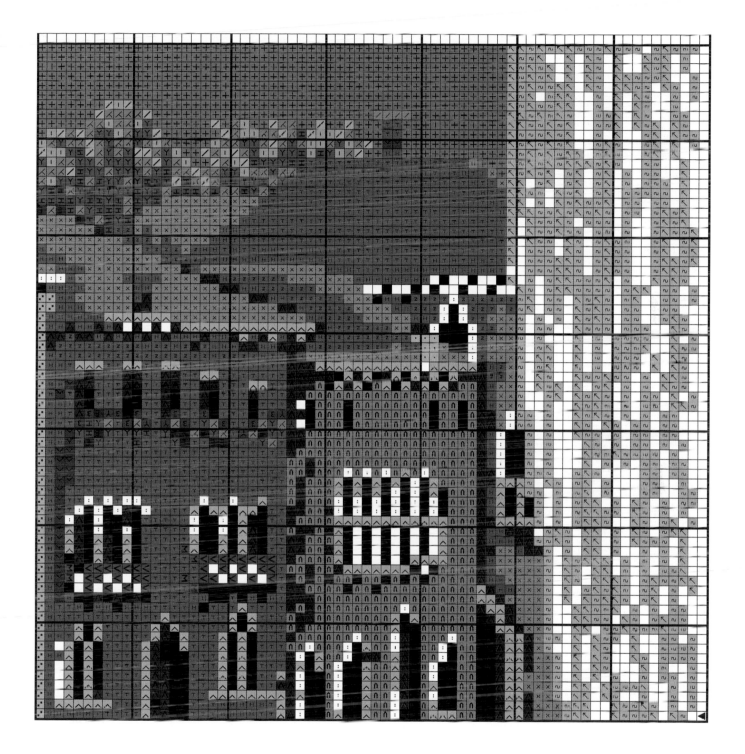

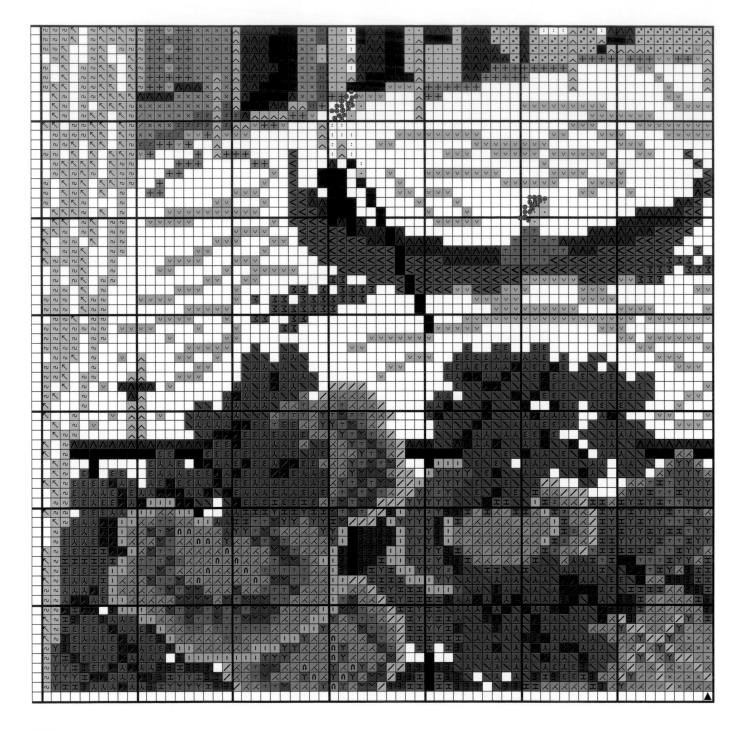

KEY
Anchor stranded
cotton (floss)

:	2	ℛ	103	/	254	▪	260	T	337	3	779	z	883	▲	8581
◣	11	v	167	✕	255	I	265	▼	338	∧	830	<	978	/	9575
◼	13	+	168	Y	256	Ɛ	332	↖	342	∩	874	•	1010	French knots
◤	20	⅃	246	⊥	257	人	333	H	379	✕	882	◼	1041	◓	1041

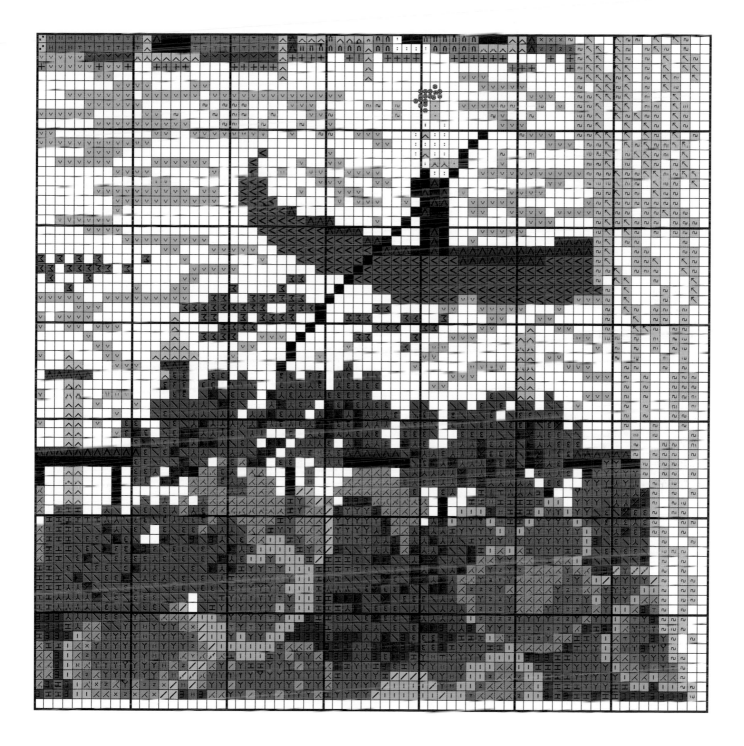

Materials and Equipment

I have always kept my stitching apparatus to a minimum, which means for me, fabric, needle, scissors and threads (plus sketchpad and pencil for any design ideas). This all fits neatly into a bag which I carry with me on most occasions so that any spare moments can be used either stitching or drawing, or making notes for future designs.

FABRIC

I have used a 14-count (14 holes per 1in/2.5cm) Aida fabric or similar count linen for all the designs in this book simply for ease of use and for the good colour range offered. Any of the designs can be stitched on evenweave, linen or a similar fabric. If you change the gauge of the material, that is the number of holes or threads per inch, then the size of the finished work will alter accordingly. If you change to an evenweave or linen fabric remember to work over two fabric threads instead of one block of Aida.

THREADS

I have chosen to use Anchor stranded embroidery cotton (floss), with some Anchor Marlitt and Kreinik thread for the projects as they offer an excellent range of colours and are generally tangle-free and easy to use. However, there is a thread conversion table on page 105 which gives equivalent DMC stranded cotton (floss) colour codes.

Two strands of stranded embroidery cotton (floss) have been used throughout, the exception being for the French knots. The skeins of stranded cotton (floss) consist of six strands and can easily be split into separate threads.

Anchor Marlitt strands can also be split and I have used two threads throughout for the cross stitches, although one strand of Anchor Marlitt consists of four threads not six.

The Kreinik threads I've used are ones in an exciting range of metallic threads and I have used their Very Fine Braids (#4) in places in the Woodcutter's Cottage design. It is available from Coats Crafts UK (see Suppliers).

NEEDLES

I find it best to use tapestry needles for cross stitch as they have a rounded point and do not snag the material. They come in many different sizes and it is a matter of preference which size you use as long as the eye is big enough to accommodate the threads of embroidery cotton (floss) easily. I have suggested size 24 or 26 but if you find these too small, you could try a 22. Needles are nickel-plated or gold-plated – the latter being much smoother to work with.

NEEDLEWORK FRAMES

Whether you use a frame or not for your stitching is a matter of personal preference. I started stitching when I was working with Kaffe Fassett and frames were not in evidence at all. Speed was always of the essence and, generally speaking, it is possible to work much faster without a frame. Personally, I find it less cumbersome and easier to work without a frame but the main thing is that you stitch in the way most enjoyable to you.

If you choose to work without a frame, be sure to watch your tension so that the work does not become distorted by uneven pulling of threads. If it does become distorted it can be restored to the proper dimensions by stretching afterwards.

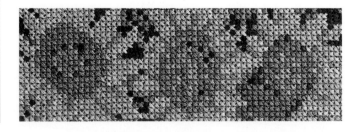

Techniques

Cross stitch embroidery requires few complicated techniques but your stitching will look its best if you follow a few simple guidelines.

PREPARING THE FABRIC

Before commencing stitching, you should make sure that your fabric is at least 5cm (2in) larger all the way round than the finished size of the stitching, as this allows for making up. Check carefully the Design Size given at the beginning of each project and make sure that this tallies with the finished size that you require for your finished piece. For instance if you get a firescreen that is larger than the one shown in the book, then be sure to measure it and to buy sufficient fabric plus at least 2in (5cm) all the way round for mounting the finished piece.

Before beginning, it is a good idea to neaten the edges of the fabric either by hemming or zigzagging to stop the fabric fraying as you work.

MARKING THE CENTRE OF THE FABRIC

Regardless of which direction you are going to work the design from, it is important to find the centre point of the fabric in order to place the work centrally on the fabric. To find the centre, fold the fabric in half horizontally and then vertically, then tack (baste) along the folds. The centre point is where the two lines of tacking (basting) meet. Alternatively, you could use tailor's chalk to mark the lines. This point on the fabric corresponds to the centre point marked on the chart. These tacked (basted) or chalk-marked lines should be removed on completion of the work.

USING A THREAD ORGANIZER

It is a good idea to sort your thread colours carefully in good natural daylight and put them on a sorter card or organizer. You could use one of the commercially available organizers or make your own by using a hole punch to cut holes down the sides of a long piece of stiff card. Each shade to be used is then threaded through a hole with the appropriate chart symbol and colour number next to each thread. This will also make it easier to work by spotlight or daylight bulb in the evenings.

USING THE CHARTS

The charts in this book are extremely clear to work from as they include symbols as well as colour blocks, making it easy to discriminate between close shades. Each square on the chart represents one stitch. Each complete chart has arrows at the sides to help you find the centre point easily. In most cases the charts have been split over several pages, with the key repeated on each double page. You may find it useful to photocopy the charts and tape the parts together. Numbering every tenth grid line (the thicker lines) is also a good idea as it will make counting easier.

STARTING AND FINISHING STITCHING

Using knots when starting and finishing will make your work lumpy. Instead, leave a 'tail' of about 3cm (1¼in) at the back and secure it by working the first few stitches over it. To finish, pass the needle through some nearby stitches on the wrong side, first in one direction and then another before cutting the thread.

WORKING THE STITCHES

All the designs are stitched principally with whole cross stitches and French knots. Try to work in such a way that you don't rub stitches already completed.

Cross Stitch

Cross stitch can be worked in two ways. A complete stitch can be worked singly (see Fig 1a) or you can sew a number of half stitches in a row and complete them on the return journey (see Fig 1b). Cross stitch worked on Aida fabric is usually worked over one block. On an evenweave or linen, you should work the cross stitches over two fabric threads to ensure they are the same size.

To make a single cross stitch over one block of Aida, bring the needle up through the fabric at the bottom right-hand side of the stitch (number 1 on Fig 1) and cross diagonally to the top left-hand corner (2). Push the needle through the hole there and bring it up at the bottom left-hand corner (3), crossing diagonally to the top right-hand corner to finish the stitch (4). To work the next stitch, push the needle up at the bottom

left-hand corner of the first stitch and repeat the steps.

To work a line of cross stitches, stitch the first part of the stitch as above and repeat along the row until the end. Complete the crosses on the way back. Always finish with the top stitches lying in the same direction.

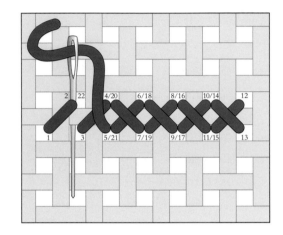

Fig 1b   Cross stitch worked in rows

French Knot

French knots have been used as the hair in the Venetian View. To work, follow Fig 2, bringing the needle up through the fabric at the exact place where the knot is to be positioned (1). Wrap the thread twice around the needle, hold the thread firmly close to it and twist the needle back through the fabric as close as possible to where it first emerged (2). Holding the knot down, pull the thread through to the back, leaving the knot on the surface; secure with a small stitch on the back.

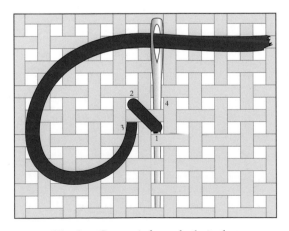

Fig 1a   Cross stitch worked singly

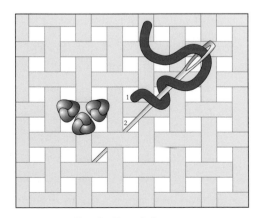

Fig 2   French knots

Making Up

There are countless ways to display cross stitch embroidery and you will no doubt have your own favourites. Below, I describe the main ways that the projects in this book have been made up.

WASHING AND IRONING EMBROIDERY

If it becomes necessary to wash your stitching, first make sure it is colourfast, then wash by hand with a gentle cleanser in tepid water. Squeeze gently but don't rub or wring. Rinse in plenty of cold or tepid water and allow to dry naturally.

To iron your work, use a medium to hot setting on a steam iron and cover the ironing board with a thick layer of towelling. Place your stitching on this, right side down, and press the fabric gently to avoid flattening the stitches.

FRAMING A DESIGN WITH FABRIC

Many designs are beautifully enhanced by being framed with complementary fabrics. Choose these fabrics carefully and decide how deep you would like the fabric borders to be. It is useful to take the embroidery with you when choosing fabrics so that you can hold the colours against the design.

Measure the length of each side of the embroidery and add on at each end the depth of the border plus a seam allowance. Cut the four strips needed, centre them and machine stitch them to the embroidery, stitching as close to the work as possible and making sure that the machine stitching of each side meets at the corners of the embroidery exactly. When you have done this, fold the work in half diagonally with the wrong sides together. You can then mitre the corners by stitching a line from the corner of the embroidery to the corner of the border panels. Do this on each corner and then trim the excess. Follow the same instructions for each fabric border that you wish to put on.

MAKING UP CUSHIONS AND PILLOWS

To make your stitching up into a cushion or pillow, choose a backing fabric which complements the stitching or, if you are going to frame the stitching with fabric, be sure that it tones with that material too. This is even more important if you are going to use the backing material for making your own piping. You will also need a cushion pad of the correct size.

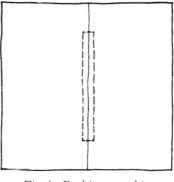

Fig 1 Backing a cushion

Cut the backing fabric using the finished work (plus the fabric frame if you are using one) as a guide, adding a further seam allowance of 1.5cm (⅝in) all the way round. (If you are using piping or cording, see page 102 overleaf.) If you are going to use a zip fastener, cut the backing fabric piece in two, adding an extra seam allowance on each half for the zip (see Fig 1 above). Insert the zip in the centre back by stitching the top and the bottom and tacking (basting) the remainder. Insert the zip in the tacked (basted) part of the seam and carefully machine it in. Then, with the right sides together, pin the backing to the embroidery. Machine stitch this in place as close as possible to the stitching, or to the appropriate edges of the material framing the stitching.

If you have inserted a zip as above, machine all four edges, otherwise machine three sides and part of the fourth. After you have inserted the cushion pad, slip stitch the part of the fourth side not already stitched.

ADDING PIPING

Edging a cushion or pillow with piping cord gives a good finishing touch. To make piping cord with the same fabric as the backing, simply buy sufficient cord and cut bias strips of fabric wide enough to cover the cord with a seam allowance of 1.25cm (½in). You may have to join the strips of fabric together to make the required length (see Fig 2). To do this, press the seams of the join open before covering the cord. Fold the strips around the piping cord and tack (baste) into place close to the cord. Pin the piping to the right side of the embroidery so that the raw edges of the piping and the material are together. Pin and tack (baste) the backing fabric to the stitching (or the material framing it) by putting the right sides together, sandwiching the piping between and machine as above. Clip the corners diagonally and turn the right way out.

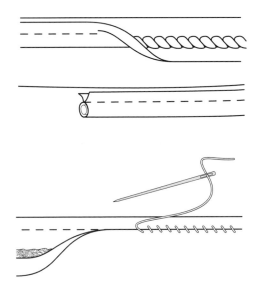

Fig 2 Making and attaching piping

MAKING UP INTO A FIRESCREEN

There are many picture framers now who are willing to mount embroideries into firescreens but if you wish to do it yourself then you will need some thin plywood or hardboard slightly smaller than the aperture of the firescreen. Centre your embroidery on the hardboard and check that it fits the aperture properly and is straight. Place the embroidery face down on some clean material and fasten it in place by lacing the back, stapling or taping it. Place the embroidery into the firescreen and put the backing board on. Most firescreens are supplied with a filler board and a backing board.

MAKING UP INTO A FOOTSTOOL

There are many upholsterers to whom you can take your finished work but if you prefer to do it yourself please read on. Most footstools are supplied with a rectangular domed piece of foam around which you can lace your finished work.

Start by carefully laying your finished work face down on some clean material or paper, then put the dome centrally on top of your stitching and draw around the perimeter of the dome with some tailor's chalk. Remove the dome and draw another line 5cm (2in) outside the first line. Then carefully cut out round the second line.

When you have trimmed your fabric loosely, tack (baste) two lines of stitching 1.25cm (½in) and 2cm (¾in) in from the edge. Leave a 15cm (6in) tail of thread at the beginning and end of the tacking (basting) on both lines so that you can use these to pull on and to draw the material in. Find the centre of the embroidery on the right side and gently pin it to the centre of the dome. Smooth the embroidery gently from the middle out towards the sides and pin in a few places. Then put the dome down on some clean material or paper and, using the drawn threads, gather the fabric in on the underside of the dome. When you are satisfied that it is smooth and tight enough, tack (baste) or staple the material to the underside of the dome. It is then ready to place into the footstool and be admired!

MAKING UP INTO A PICTURE

You could take your finished work to a picture framer and choose the mount board and frame you like or you can do the whole thing yourself. If you choose to do the latter, then you will need a box for cutting mitred edges on frames, some panel pins, a suitable saw, some hardboard (or thick card) and mount board. When choosing mount board, it is helpful to hold the edges of the mount board next to your finished work, with the frame at the outer edge to get the best idea of what the end result will be.

Mount your embroidery on to some thin hardboard or card and fasten in place by lacing it around the card or by stapling it. Decide on the frame size you require and carefully cut your frame pieces to the correct size, then panel pin them together. Using a mount cutter (which is by far the easiest) or a craft or Stanley knife, cut your mount board to the required depth. Place the mount board into the frame, then the embroidery. Finally, cut hardboard to size for the backing and wedge it in with metal clips.

MAKING UP A WALL HANGING OR RUNNER
A wall hanging is a lovely way to display embroidery, while a runner is perfect for adorning a table top, chest of drawers or sideboard. If you wish to frame the stitched work with fabric borders, follow the instructions on page 101.

Wall hangings or runners can be backed with a suitable fabric which is best attached by slip stitching on to the embroidery (see Fig 3). Personally, I think it is much more fun to frame them with fabric and even to embroider into the designs on the fabric.

If you are using interfacing or wadding (batting), attach it by tacking (basting) it on to the wrong side of the stitching and fabric frames. The backing is then placed on the stitching, with right sides together. Machine all three sides and part of the fourth, then turn the fabric right way out and slip stitch the remaining part of the fourth side.

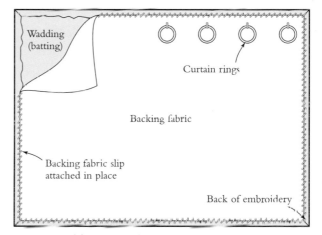

Fig 3 Making a wall hanging

To hang the wall hanging, attach curtain rings at regular intervals at a depth of 4cm–5cm (1½in–2in) from the top of the hanging on the wrong side. If you prefer you can make stitched loops. Simply slide a curtain rod or length of wooden dowling through these to suspend it from the wall, from cup hooks or other suitable fastenings.

ACKNOWLEDGMENTS

My sincerest thanks go to Sally Jefferson at Coats Crafts UK for her enthusiasm, help and support for my work. This resulted in Coats supplying all the embroidery threads for the book and many of the fabrics and also supplying some of the stitchers, and I am extremely thankful to them for all of their help. A special thanks to Michaela Learner, one of Coats' stitchers, who must have eight hands to stitch so quickly and who does such beautiful work.

Warmest thanks go to Penelope Williams at Lady Penelope Needlecrafts who has become a very good friend to me and has helped so wonderfully with the firescreen, footstool and framing – and who has also provided excellent stitchers. Many thanks also to Fabric Flair for supplying many colours of Aida fabric.

Thanks also to Cheryl Brown at David & Charles for her encouragement and input in producing this book. And last but by no means least I owe a huge debt of gratitude to Lin Clements, who has not only been a truly wonderful editor but also a huge support in pressing times!

Suppliers

KIT SUPPLIER
Millennia Designs
Prospect Cottage, The Street,
Crookham Village,
Hampshire UK, GU13 0SH
tel: 01252 616369
www.millennia.demon.co.uk
*Many of Jill Gordon's designs are
available as cross stitch and needlepoint
kits from Millennia Designs. Please write
or telephone for brochure and information
or visit the website. Millennia Designs
also supply general needlework materials
and ship worldwide.*

THREAD SUPPLIER
Coats Crafts UK
PO Box 22, Lingfield,
McMullen Road, Darlington
County Durham UK, DL1 1YQ
tel: 01325 394242
fax: 01325 368822
*Suppliers of all the threads used in the
book and many of the fabrics.*

FABRIC SUPPLIERS
Coats Crafts UK (as above)
Fabric Flair
for nearest stockist/shop contact:
Solo Designs
tel: 0845 126 0773
email: enquiries@solocrafts.com
OR freephone 0800 731 4563
email: info@fabricflair.com
www.fabricflair.com

FRAME AND FOOTSTOOL
SUPPLIER
Lady Penelope's Needlecrafts
8 Station Road, Parkstone
Poole, Dorset, UK BH14 8UB
tel: 01202 735881
email: ladyp@supanet.com
www.lady-penelope.co.uk
*Also suppliers of threads, fabrics, kits,
books and much more.*

Index

entries in **bold** type
indicate main subjects

Thread Conversion Chart

The designs in this book use Anchor stranded cottons (floss). If you wish to use DMC stranded cotton (floss), please use this conversion chart only as a guide, as exact colour comparisons between manufacturers cannot always be made, indeed some colours have no direct comparison. If you wish to use Madeira threads, telephone for their conversion chart on 01845 524880 or e mail: acts@madeira.co.uk

Anchor	DMC	Anchor	DMC	Anchor	DMC	Anchor	DMC	Anchor	DMC	Anchor	DMC
1	B5200	175	794	265	471	366	739	877	502	1022	760
2	white	186	959	266	470	367	422	878	501	1023	3712
9	352	189	943	267	469	368	3828	882	754	1024	3328
10	351	203	954	268	937	369	729	885	613	1025	347
11	350	204	912	269	935	371	780	886	3046	1028	816
13	349	206	564	273	645	374	420	887	371	1037	3756
33	892	208	563	274	928	375	869	888	370	1038	519
35	891	209	910	277	830	380	898	889	610	1039	518
45	814	210	562	279	734	381	938	890	729	1040	647
49	3689	212	561	280	733	382	3371	891	676	1041	844
60	3688	215	320	281	581	387	ecru	897	221	1042	542
68	3687	216	367	289	307	388	3024	898	611	1043	369
69	3803	225	702	290	973	403	310	901	680	1044	319
77	3350	226	702	295	726	410	995	904	3787	1047	402
92	552	227	701	298	972	433	996	905	3021	1048	3776
98	553	236	413	300	745	683	500	926	613	1049	301
99	552	238	703	302	743	817	937	927	3755	1062	598
100	208	240	966	303	742	843	3053	944	869	1064	597
118	340	241	704	304	741	845	730	945	833	1066	3810
119	333	242	989	305	725	846	936	956	3047	1070	993
131	3807	244	987	306	3820	851	924	1001	976	1072	992
134	820	245	699	307	783	853	3013	1002	977	1074	3814
140	3755	246	986	308	781	854	370	1003	921	1076	991
142	798	253	472	309	780	855	3012	1004	920	1088	838
145	799	254	472	324	721	856	936	1013	356	1094	605
146	798	255	907	326	720	861	935	1014	355	1098	3801
160	827	256	704	338	351	870	3042	1015	3777	5975	3830
167	3766	257	905	340	919	871	3041	1016	3727		
168	807	258	904	358	433	874	833	1017	316		
169	806	261	3364	363	436	875	3813	1020	3713		
170	3765	264	3348	365	435	876	503	1021	761